# Observing in Schools

# Observing in Schools

## A Guide for Students in Teacher Education

**EUGENE F. PROVENZO, JR.**
**WILLIAM E. BLANTON**
*University of Miami*

PEARSON

Boston   New York   San Francisco
Mexico City   Montreal   Toronto   London   Madrid   Munich   Paris
Hong Kong   Singapore   Tokyo   Cape Town   Sydney

**Executive Editor and Publisher:** *Stephen D. Dragin*
**Series Editorial Assistant:** *Meaghan Minnick*
**Marketing Manager:** *Tara Kelly*
**Production Editor:** *Greg Erb*
**Editorial Production Service:** *Walsh & Associates, Inc.*
**Manufacturing and Composition Buyer:** *Andrew Turso*
**Electronic Composition:** *Publishers' Design and Production Services, Inc.*
**Interior Design:** *Publishers' Design and Production Services, Inc.*
**Cover Administrator:** Joel Gendron

For related titles and support materials, visit our online catalog at www.ablongman.com.

Between the time website information is gathered and then published, it is not unusual for some sites to have closed. Also, the transcription of URLs can result in typographical errors. The publisher would appreciate notification where these errors occur so that they may be corrected in subsequent editions.

*Library of Congress Cataloging-in-Publication Data*

Provenzo, Eugene F.
    Observing in schools : a guide for students in teacher education /
Eugene F. Provenzo, Jr., William E. Blanton.—1st ed.
        p.   cm.
    Includes bibliographical references.
    ISBN 0-205-40140-6
    1. Observation (Educational method)  2. Teachers—Training of.
I. Blanton, William E. II. Title.
LB1731.6.P76 2006
370'.71'1—dc22

                                                            2005051808

Printed in the United States of America

10  9  8  7  6  5  4  3  2  1  CIN  09  08  07  06  05

# Contents

# Preface

This book is intended to provide students in teacher education with the basic skills and background they need to conduct field-based observations and research in schools and related educational settings. It can be used at the undergraduate and masters levels for people entering the teaching profession.

We feel strongly that conducting careful and systematic field-based observations and interviews is essential to the education of teachers. Our approach is based on well-established traditions of anthropology and sociology, as well as more recent models from the field of cultural studies. We are drawn, in particular, to the work of Henry Giroux, who argues that teachers in a complex postmodern culture such as the contemporary United States need to understand that schools are ". . . border institutions in which teachers, students, and others engage in daily acts of cultural translation and negotiation" (Giroux, 1997, p. 239). According to Giroux:

> . . . border pedagogy offers the opportunity for students to engage the multiple references that constitute different cultural codes, experiences and languages. This means educating students to both read these codes historically and critically while simultaneously learning the limits of such codes, including the ones they use to construct their own narratives and histories. (Giroux, 1994, p. 29)

As "border crossers" (Giroux, 1992, p. 28), teachers need to think more like anthropologists than scientists, more like explorers than technicians. There are many skills necessary to be a border crosser. You must learn to carefully observe. You must learn to listen. You must reflect on what you see.

This book will provide you with the basic tools to begin to become a border crosser, a critical and reflective observer and interviewer, and, most important, a better teacher. We hope that you will find it helpful in dealing with the complex and challenging settings found in contemporary schools.

Eugene F. Provenzo, Jr. and William E. Blanton
*Staunton, Virginia*
*Miami, Florida*

# Acknowledgments

**W**e would like to acknowledge the many people who have helped us in the creation of this book. Our main thanks go to our colleagues in the Department of Teaching and Learning, School of Education, University of Miami. In particular, we would like to thank Jeanne Schumm for her leadership in curriculum reform and her efforts to help us be the best that we can be as scholars, teachers, and members of our larger community.

We would also like to thank the following reviewers: Helen L. Carlson, University of Minnesota Duluth; Cynthia Chapel, Lincoln University; Ramona E. Patterson, South Louisiana Community College; Robert Wandberg, University of Minnesota Mankato; and Merrill K. Watrous, Lane Community College.

Asterie Baker Provenzo is thanked for her good humor, patience, and excellence as an editor. Thanks also go to Linda Blanton for her interest in our work and her commitment to the improvement of teacher education.

# For Faculty and Students Using This Book

This book is intended for use in an introductory field observation course, or as part of the field experience in a content area or methods course in education. It can also be used selectively across courses in an entire undergraduate or graduate program in education. It is based on the authors' belief that the goal of preparation for professional practice, such as teaching, is to "initiate students into 'traditions of the calling' and help them by the right kind of telling; to see on their behalf and in their own way what they need most to see" (Schon, 1987, p. 17).

To "see" and to think with content, beginning education students need to do a number of things. They need to learn to *observe, notice, notate, predict, generate, analyze, critique,* and *reflect*. We feel that these are the essential tasks required of those doing observations and fieldwork in school and classroom settings. All require beginning teacher observers to learn to monitor how they work in the field, how they use language, and how they think.

What you need to do to be an effective observer in educational settings:

1. *observe*
2. *notice*
3. *notate*
4. *predict*
5. *generate*
6. *analyze*
7. *critique*
8. *reflect*

According to Goodwin (1994), "professional vision" is a codified manner of viewing professional practice (teaching, medicine, law and legal practices, for example). Members of different professions have the power to legitimately see, constitute, formulate, and articulate different kinds of events. As an illustration, when attending a police academy, novice police officers learn how to observe and describe a crime scene.

In medical school, novice physicians learn how to view and listen to a patient for the purpose of identifying symptoms and possible causes of disease. Novice epidemiologists must learn the many ways to view and track the ontology of diseases.

Teacher education candidates often enter teacher preparation believing that they have a clear idea of what is involved in being a teacher. This is based on the fact that unlike other professions, they have spent at least a dozen years of their lives participating in and indirectly observing in K–12 schools. Much of the time, however, beginning teachers have a misconception of what schools are actually about.

For example, many beginning teachers believe that teaching is simply sequestering pupils, standing in front of a class, and handing out prepackaged knowledge that pupils must commit to memory. Typically, beginning teachers believe that teaching is largely about exposing students to content through telling, while trying to make learning interesting.

Prospective teachers also often believe that, although they tend to lack in-depth knowledge of subject matter, they already possess the qualities most meaningful for successful teaching. They believe, in large part, that the pupils they will teach in the future will behave in much the same way as they did when they were in school. Many teacher education candidates expect to be successful teachers simply because they care for children and believe they possess the everyday knowledge necessary for managing classrooms.

Such ideas are often naïve and limiting. Research suggests that despite rigorous coursework and field experiences in education, beginning teachers often hold onto their misconceptions of what "life in classrooms" is actually about. However, when given the opportunity to confront their misconceptions and subject them to critical analysis and reflection, to explore abstract course concepts in clinical settings, or to work in alternative educational programs, beginning teachers will, in fact, begin to transform their misconceptions.

We feel strongly that in order to help beginning teachers transform their misconceptions about what classrooms and the work of teachers are actually about, it is necessary to have them participate in alternative learning settings that integrate theory and practice. Such experiences are best provided by reflective fieldwork—i.e., fieldwork involving extensive observation and interview. Simply stated, pre-service teachers, and beginning teachers in general, need to learn to observe and listen, and in turn, to reflect on what it is that they have seen and heard.

The arguments outlined above reflect the basic philosophical perspective of this book. We ask both students and faculty using this text to reflect on its meaning and to use it to help in the construction or further development of approaches and philosophies for integrating fieldwork and observations into their work as educators.

About one-third of this book provides a general introduction to conducting observations and doing fieldwork in educational settings. The remaining two-thirds of the book is a collection of observation and interview forms you can take with you into the field. Our intention is to provide you with a general background and grounding for entering the field, and then give you a set of guidelines for conducting your fieldwork.

Feel free to adopt and use materials in creative ways—ways that suit your needs as classroom observers and researchers. What we have attempted to create is a starting point, a set of suggestions, for questions that will emerge from your work. Ideally, we hope to help you become not only better observers, but also more reflective practitioners.

Included in the Appendix is a three-step framework for conducting classroom observations and interviews. It is intended to be optional in use—hence its inclusion as an appendix.

# PART I
........................

# Doing Fieldwork in Education

Going into classrooms and collecting information by observing and interviewing involves a series of strategic decisions. It is also a systematic process that involves not only the collection of data, but also analysis and reflection. In *Part I: Doing Fieldwork in Education,* we provide a basic introduction to some of the practical and theoretical issues underlying fieldwork in education.

# Conducting Observation and Interview Research

*"You can observe a lot just by watching."*

—Yogi Berra

All of us participate in observation and interview research in our daily lives. Perhaps you got up this morning and looked out the window to see what the weather was like. Or maybe you asked a friend what she thought about a local election or political issue. Maybe you observed a traffic jam on the highway and decided to drive an alternate route, or you asked a friend if you looked better in one outfit or another.

Each of these examples involves either observing or interviewing. Such activities are an essential part of our day-to-day lives. Observing and interviewing are also the basis for doing fieldwork in education.

Think about the class for which you are using this book. Look at the instructor teaching in front of you. Imagine, for a moment, you are an anthropologist or sociologist observing his or her behavior. What can you learn by watching your instructor's interaction with students? How does the design or layout of the classroom affect what goes on? Do the types of clothes worn by the instructor tell you anything about his or her role or status? Do these clothes differ from what students wear? How does the instructor interact with students? Does he or she respond to different students in different ways? Why? How do different students respond to the instructor? All of a sudden, a lot of day-to-day things become very interesting.

What is happening is that you are learning about teaching as a social and cultural act—not just an educational act. You are learning by observing. Yogi Berra, the great baseball player and philosopher of life, summed it up perfectly when he explained that: "You can observe a lot just by watching."

Consider what you could learn by going back to the people you observed and asking them why they did what they did. Try to learn something about their assumptions and beliefs by interviewing them. Think about integrating the results and the results from your observations with the information you have collected from your interviews.

Go out and observe an elementary or secondary class in a local school. Compare the class you are observing and analyzing to your own school experience at the same grade level. How was your experience the same or different? If there are significant differences in what you observe (from when you were in school), what does this mean?

The process of observing and interviewing in educational settings cannot be separated from the process of asking larger questions about education and U.S. culture. If you observe carefully in any classroom setting, you must inevitably come to terms with issues of race, gender, and social class. Other issues also become evident as well.

In summary, conducting observations and interviews provides you with powerful tools for data collection—data that you can analyze to learn more about schools and classrooms as social and cultural settings—data and ideas that will help you to become a better teacher.

# Why Beginning Teachers Need to Do Fieldwork

**F**ieldwork provides what is probably the best opportunity to integrate theory and practice in your studies in education. By looking at what goes on in the real world of classrooms you can directly apply what you have been learning in your academic courses at your college or university.

By definition, fieldwork makes you a border crosser. You cannot do careful observations and interviews in classrooms and schools without dealing with different cultural codes. When you step into a classroom—even in a culture or setting that is familiar to you—you are forced to deal with alternative points of view and cultural differences. Think of yourself as a cultural geographer—you are exploring new territory.

Fieldwork potentially makes theory real by connecting it to practice. This integration of *theory* and *practice* is called *praxis*.

> Praxis: A term used by A. von Cieszkowski in *Prolegomena zur Historiosophie* (Berlin, 1838), then adopted by Karl Marx in *Zür Kritik der Hegelschen Rechtsphilosophie, Einleitung,* in the *Deutsch-Französische Jahrbücher* (1844), to denote the willed action by which a theory or philosophy (esp. a Marxist one) becomes a social actuality. Also *attrib.* and *transf.*
>
> This term, frequently translated as *practice, practical ability,* or *practical activity,* has been increasingly used since the 1960s, following the translation and availability of Marx's early writings.
>
> *Oxford English Dictionary*

Think for a moment about driving a car. To drive well, you need to understand some basic facts, including how the car runs, what fuel it uses, the rules of the road, and so on. Much of this information, which is theoretical, is probably best communicated through a written explanation or lecture.

At some point, however, you need to get beyond classroom and theoretical learning and actually drive a car. Getting behind the wheel of a car takes the process of driving beyond the realm of information and theory into practice. Prior theoretical knowledge and information combine with the practical aspects of driving to create *praxis*.

*Theory* (learning about driving) + *Practice* (actually driving) = *Praxis*

*Praxis* means making the theoretical world real through practice. For someone interested in teaching, this means taking what you have learned in your classes and what you have observed in the field and making it real through the actual act of teaching.

# Anthropology and Traditions of Observation

Observational research has a long tradition in the history of the social sciences. Systematic educational observations are based on this type of work, which has its origins in the late nineteenth century. How fieldwork is done can perhaps be best understood by looking at the work of pioneering anthropologist Franz Boas (1858–1942).

Boas, perhaps the most famous anthropologist working in the United States at the beginning of the twentieth century, studied the Kwakiutl in British Columbia, Canada. From his research he concluded that everything was important in the study of a culture—not just the formal, but also the informal.

Kwakiutl village, with totem poles, Alert Bay, British Columbia, c. 1914. Courtesy of the Library of Congress.

Look at the following excerpt from Franz Boas's 1895 report on the social organization and secret societies of the Kwakiutl. Consider the richness of what he is describing in terms of the characteristics and conditions of the culture he is observing. Think about how Boas's description lets you begin to create an image or picture of Kwakiutl culture and society. Imagine yourself being an anthropologist and studying something in U.S. culture such as a shopping mall or a high school. Could you construct an equally rich or "thick" description?

While a hasty glance at these people and a comparison with other tribes emphasize the uniformity of their culture, a closer investigation reveals many peculiarities of individual tribes which prove that their culture has developed slowly and from a number of distinct centers, each people adding something to the culture which we observe at the present day. . . .

In the woods the deer, the elk, the black and grizzly bear, the wolf and many other animals are found. The mountain goat lives on the higher ranges of the mainland. The beaver, the otter, marten mink, and fur seal furnish valuable skins, which were formerly used for blankets. The Indians keep in their villages dogs which assist the hunters.

The staple food of the Indians is, however, furnished by the sea: Seals, sea lions, and whales are found in considerable numbers; but people depend almost entirely upon various species of salmon, the halibut, and the oulachon or candlefish (*Thaleichthys pacificus,* Girard), which are caught in enormous quantities. Various specimens of cod and other sea fish also furnish food. Herrings visit the coast early in spring. In short, there is such an abundance of animal life in the sea that the Indians live almost solely upon it. Besides fish, they gather various kinds of shellfish, sea urchins and cuttlefish.

Qa hila, a Koprino man, bust portrait, facing front, with bone in nose, c. 1914. Courtesy of the Library of Congress.

The people are, therefore, essentially fishermen, all other pursuits being of secondary importance. Whales are pursued only by the tribes of the west coast of Vancouver Islands. Other tribes are satisfied with the dead carcasses of whales which drift ashore. Sea lions, like seals, are harpooned, and the barged harpoon point either attached to a bladder or tied to the stern of the canoe. The harpoon lines are made of cedar bark and sinews. The meat of these sea animals is eaten, while their intestines are used for the manufacture of bowstrings and bags. . . .

The natives of this region go bare legged. The principal part of their clothing is the blanket, and this was made of tanned skins or woven mountain-goat wool, dog's hair, feathers, or a mixture of both. The thread is spun on the bare leg and by means of a spindle. Another kind of blanket is made of soft cedar bark, the warp being tied across the weft. These blankets are trimmed with fur. At the present time woolen blankets are more extensively used.

At festive occasions "button blankets" are worn. Most of these are light blue blankets with a red border set with mother of pearl buttons. Many are also adorned with the crest of the owner, which is cut of red cloth and sewed on to the blanket. Men wear a shirt under the blanket, while women wear a petticoat in addition.

Tsawatenok girl, head-and-shoulders portrait, facing front, c. 1914. Courtesy of the Library of Congress.

Before the introduction of woolen blankets, women used to wear an apron made of cedar bark and a belt made of the same material. When canoeing or working on the beach, the women wear large water-tight hats made of basketry. In rainy weather, a water-tight cape or poncho made of cedar bark is used. The women dress their hair in two plaits, while the men wear it cooperatively short. The latter keep it back from the face by means of a strap of fur or cloth tied around the head. Ear and nose ornaments are used extensively. They are made of bone and abalone shell. The women of the most northern tribes (from Skeena River northward) wear labrets.

A great variety of baskets are used—large wicker baskets favor carrying fish and clams, cedar-bark baskets for purposes of storage. Mats made of cedar bark, and in the south such bake *[sic]* of rushes are used for bedding, packing seats, dishes, covers of boxes, and similar purposes.

*Source: Franz Boas, The Indian Tribes of the North Pacific Coast, excerpted from "The Social Organization and the Secret Societies of the Kwakiutl Indians," Report of the U.S. National Museum for 1895, pages 317–22.*

# Observing and Noticing Things
..................................................

*"The way we see things is affected by what we know or what we believe."*

—John Berger

Teaching is one of the few professions that people have extensive experience with prior to their professional training. The average student, by the time he or she has completed twelfth grade, will have spent approximately 13,000 hours in a classroom setting. In other professions, such as law, medicine, and engineering, students have virtually no prior experience before they begin their education and training.

As a result, people entering the teaching profession have a tendency to confirm their prior knowledge, rather than see or learn things anew. A beginning doctor, learning a surgical procedure, will bring fewer assumptions to what he or she is observing than a beginning teacher, who has had at least a dozen years of experience in classrooms.

Most prospective teachers come to university education courses with deeply rooted ideas about teaching and learning, largely shaped by their own experiences as students in classes that offered traditional instruction. Learning to teach successfully in a way that is consistent with current education reforms means that you must transform your understanding and conceptions of teaching, learning, development, and subject matter (e.g., Carpenter, Fennema, Peterson, & Carey, 1988; Cohen & Ball, 1990; Thompson, 1984). The knowledge, skills, and dispositions necessary to teach in the manner advocated by reform movements require a significantly different experience in schools than what you probably found during your early education.

We believe that a foundational skill that underpins participating in classrooms during university methods courses is the ability to recognize and interpret classroom activity. Recall the eight essential tasks we outlined earlier that are required for doing observations and fieldwork in school and classroom settings: *observe, notice, notate, predict, generate, analyze, critique,* and *reflect.* These activities provide the basic the toolkit used for critical analysis and reflection for learning to teach.

The fact that beginning teachers bring their experience as students to their work as teachers is further complicated by the fact that teaching is widely portrayed—often inaccurately—in popular culture sources such as television and the movies. Thus, beginning, and even experienced teachers, have to overcome myths and stereotypes about the profession that are promoted through electronic media. Michelle Pfeiffer, for example, in the film *Dangerous Minds* (1995), portrays a teacher in a challenging urban/multicultural setting. She would never be able to actually do half of the things she does as a teacher in the movie (take students on a field trip without the permission of the school and parents; have a male student stay overnight with her as a single woman in her apartment in order to protect him; and so on). Yet Pfeiffer and *Dangerous Minds* are regularly referred to beginning teachers as providing a model for their work.

The Italian social theorist Antonio Gramsci (1891–1937) once made the comment that people in their day-to-day lives are like fish in an aquarium who never notice the water that is all around them. People likewise take for granted the social institutions such as schools that are so much a part of their daily lives. As a result, when beginning, or even experienced, teachers are asked to observe schools, they often fail to see everything that is there. Observing at a deep and meaningful level is not automatic. Good field observers see beyond the immediate and familiar to the deeper level of things that are around them.

An example from most people's experience comes to mind. Were you involved in a reading group when you were younger in which each student was invited by the teacher to answer a question? Typically, each student responded, and the teacher evaluated the question as right or wrong. Did you ever think about what was being learned? What you might have been learning was that the purpose of reading is to be able to answer questions rather than understand and interpret what you read. Research shows that this method of interrogation to teach comprehension is not very effective from an instructional point of view (Durkin, 1978–79).

The reality is that students do not focus on the meaning of what they are reading. Instead, they are anticipating the answers to questions. This kind of instruction is called an *Invite, Student Responds, Teacher Evaluates Sequence*. The result is that students are not really engaged with the text or the learning process until it is their turn to read. Careful systematic observations—combined with interviews—make it clear that *Round Robin Question-Asking* reading is largely ineffective. Simply accepting the use of this method, without critically observing what actually takes place, leads to poor instruction. A more helpful questioning routine is for the teacher to follow up on students' answers to questions with more discussion. This routine is called an *Invite, Student Responds, Teacher Follows Up Sequence*.

Your job as an observer—whether you are taking field notes on the side or are teaching yourself—is to notice what is actually going on in the classroom. Are actual learning and participation taking place, or are students simply going through the motions? We believe that careful critical observation of what occurs in the classroom determines the extent to which teachers will, in fact, be successful in instruction.

# Observing Language

The use of language often provides important clues about what is going on in a classroom or educational setting. Listen, for example, to how language is used in mixed gender settings. Are masculine terms such as "you guys" or "mankind" consistently emphasized?

What types of metaphors or similes are used to describe things? Are sports metaphors emphasized, for example, in terms of talking about working together? Are students asked to "work as a team," or "pull together"? Is the work of women described differently than the work of men? For example, is a girl's poem or drawing described as being "sweet" or "cute," while a boy's work is described as "thoughtful" and "interesting"?

Think about metaphors that are larger than the ones used above. For example, the *classroom metaphor* suggests that instruction is what goes on in classrooms during 50-minute intervals. Following this way of thinking, instruction and learning are what happens in schools. The emphasis is often on the teacher's presentation and related activities, since so much school-based instruction is teacher-led and teacher-centered. In everyday language, our use of "instruction" often rests on the classroom metaphor. Look at the following metaphors and what they imply:

- Stakeholders hold the stakes for a race
- Students as multitaskers
- Teaching is telling
- Learning is listening
- Inside a student's head
- In the teacher's head
- Classrooms as war zones
- Schools as zoos
- Communities of practice
- Poor attending

Now, think about the following:

| *If you think of knowledge as . . .* | *Then you may tend to think of instruction as . . .* |
| --- | --- |
| a quantity or packet of content waiting to be transmitted | a product to be delivered by a vehicle |
| a cognitive state as reflected in a person's schemas and procedural skills | a set of instructional strategies aimed at changing an individual's schemas |
| a person's meanings constructed by interaction with one's environment | a learner drawing on tools and resources within a rich environment |
| enculturation or adoption of a group's ways of seeing and acting | participation in a community's everyday activities |

Use your observations of language to determine the values and beliefs of the people whom you are observing. Reflect on how your own values and beliefs are illustrated in the terms you use every day.

# Observing Authority and Power

**E**lementary and secondary teachers are responsible for large numbers of students. In managing their classrooms and what they are teaching, they must assume a certain degree of authority. Educational philosopher Kenneth Benne argues that there are three types of authority: *the authority of expertise (skill or knowledge in a specific field), the authority of rules (guidelines for action and behavior in a specific activity— i.e. the rules of baseball game),* and *the authority of community* (Benne, 1943). The point is that schools and authority are not necessarily benign or neutral.

For Benne, the authority of community is most important to the work of teachers. Only through a knowledge of the skills, information, and values of a community can a teacher obtain authority. This is why a teacher who has authority in a private religious school may not have the same type of authority if he or she moves to a setting such as a public school.

Authority can be physical. It can involve a teacher's literally imposing his or her authority through tone of voice, physical force (pulling two students apart in a fight), or size (kindergarten teachers loom as giants over young children).

Teachers can exercise their authority through the imposition of moral values based on rules or traditions. In elite private schools in the United States, these values can manifest themselves in the form of specific moral or ethical codes.

Teachers also have authority as a result of affection and respect they may have earned by working with people. This type of authority is typically earned by a teacher with each class he or she teaches and is not automatically carried from class to class or year to year.

Finally, teachers obtain authority from being expert in a subject matter. This is particularly true of high school and college teachers, whose work by definition is more subject oriented.

As you spend time observing in different classrooms and educational settings, pay particular attention to how authority functions.

Authority is closely related to the concept of power. Individuals with authority are often assigned power (the power to punish, to give a failing grade, etc.). Power is also exercised over those with authority. Thus, a teacher can be subject to the power of his or her principal, to the power of parents, or to the power of a local school board and community.

Think about authority and power in the schools you have attended. Who held authority? Who held power? How did they work? Did certain students have authority? Did certain students have power? Why? How did it work?

# On the Non-Neutrality of the Observer

*"Natural science does not simply describe and explain nature; it is part of the interplay between nature and ourselves; it describes nature as exposed to our method of questioning."*

—Werner Hesienberg

There is a great deal of discussion in academic circles about people being "scientific," "neutral," and "objective" observers. We believe that it is impossible for anyone to be totally objective or neutral in the process of conducting observations. None of us can entirely escape our personal history and experience. We inevitably bring something of who we are to the process of observation.

Despite this fact, we can step back from what we are doing sufficiently to be reasonably objective. Neither of the two authors of this book, for example, are women, nor are we African American, but despite this fact we should be able to understand and describe—perhaps imperfectly—the experience of a female African American teacher working in a classroom setting.

As observers and interviewers, we must be very clear about where we are coming from. We must not only understand that we bring ourselves and our personal perspective to what we study, but also that through the process of observation we potentially change and alter what is being studied.

School settings cannot be viewed as benign or neutral places for being introduced to teaching. Most school communities do not foster risk taking, inquiry, reflection, and the transformation of practice (McLaughlin & Talbert, 1993). The policies of schools are often translated into pedagogical practices that fossilize what is assumed about pupils, what is taught, how it is taught, and what counts as acceptable teacher and pupil performance (Knapp, Gallucci, & Markholt, 2000). The concerns of schools are mirrored in the language of classroom teachers and determine what teaching and learning artifacts are put on public display in the classroom and hallways of schools, providing a lens through which teacher education students can construct the meaning of pupils and classroom teaching (Grossman, Valencia, & Thompson, 2000).

Beginning teachers need to be able to step back from the classrooms in which they are working and ask questions about how and why they function the way they do. Careful observation and interviewing can provide the tools by which to clarify what they see.

## Creating an Individual School or District Profile

**W**henever you conduct a set of observations in a school or classroom setting, it is critically important to be able to contextualize your findings. This means that you must try to understand the school or classroom you are observing in the context of its neighborhood, the social and economic class of the students attending it, its racial and ethnic composition, and so on.

In a place such as Miami, Florida, there are enormous differences between schools based on the factors described above. In a Miami suburb called Pinecrest, for example (which has one of the highest per capita incomes for families in the state), parents of students are either highly successful business people or high-income professionals, such as doctors and lawyers. The area is heavily populated with White Anglos and elite Hispanics. Expectations from parents are extremely high. It is assumed that students will go on to college and high-level careers.

In contrast, about ten miles north of Pinecrest, near downtown Miami, is the neighborhood known as "Little Haiti." This is a community of Haitian immigrants, many of them illegal boat people. The socioeconomic level of the community is very low, as are the educational expectations of parents. The parents of the children attending the schools speak little English. They work at entry-level jobs in the economic system (day laborers, maids, short order cooks, etc.).

What goes on in each school is very much shaped by its community. In Little Haiti, parents rarely challenge the authority of the school. They often expect teachers to physically discipline their children. In contrast, in the suburban Pinecrest neighborhood, it is far less likely that parents would tolerate their children being physically disciplined. Parents feel it is their obligation and duty to challenge educational practices they do not agree with.

How can you find out about the social characteristics of a school where you are doing observations? Most school districts will have extensive printed and online profiles available on not only the overall district, but individual schools as well. For example, in Miami, individual school profiles can be found at the Miami/Dade County Public Schools site: http://www.dadeschools.net/

Use a search engine such as Google or Yahoo to find websites with information about your local school system or individual schools. If you were looking for profiles on the Miami/Dade County Public Schools, for example, you could type into a search engine "School Profiles, Miami/Dade County." Experiment with searching for information on other school districts, including those near where you live or attend a college or university.

Many state departments of education also provide links to local school districts and actual school sites. Visit your state department of education to see whether it includes links to schools in your part of the country. You should also find a wide range of additional information at state websites that may prove helpful to you in your work in education. A list of state department of education websites follows.

## State Department of Education Websites

**Alabama**
http://alaweb.asc.edu/

**Alaska**
http://www.state.ak.us/

**Arizona**
http://www.state.az.us/

**Arkansas**
http://www.state.ar.us/

**California**
http://www.ca.gov/

**Colorado**
http://www.state.co.us/

**Delaware**
http://www.state.de.us/

**Florida**
http://www.state.fl.us/gsd/

**Georgia**
http://www.state.ga.us/

**Hawaii**
http://www.state.hi.us/

**Idaho**
http://www.accessidaho.org/
index.html

**Illinois**
http://www.state.il.us/

**Indiana**
http://www.state.in.us/

**Iowa**
http://www.state.ia.us/

**Kansas**
http://www.state.ks.us/

**Kentucky**
http://www.state.ky.us/

**Louisiana**
http://www.state.la.us/

**Maine**
http://www.state.me.us/

**Maryland**
http://www.mec.state.md.us/

**Massachusetts**
http://www.state.ma.us/

**Michigan**
http://www.migov.state.mi.us/

**Minnesota**
http://www.state.mn.us/

**Mississippi**
http://www.state.ms.us

**Missouri**
http://www.state.mo.us/

Nebraska
http://www.state.ne.us/

Nevada
http://www.state.nv.us/

New Hampshire
http://www.state.nh.us/

New Jersey
http://www.state.nj.us/

New Mexico
http://www.state.nm.us/

New York
http://www.state.ny.us/

North Carolina
http://www.state.nc.us/

North Dakota
http://www.state.nd.us/

Ohio
http://www.state.oh.us/

Oklahoma
http://www.state.ok.us/

Oregon
http://www.state.or.us/

Pennsylvania
http://www.state.pa.us/

Rhode Island
http://www.info.state.ri.us/

South Carolina
http://www.state.sc.us/

South Dakota
http://www.state.sd.us/

Tennessee
http://www.state.tn.us/

Texas
http://www.state.tx.us/

Utah
http://www.state.ut.us/

Vermont
http://www.cit.state.vt.us/

Virginia
http://www.state.va.us/

Washington
http://www.state.wa.us/

West Virginia
http://www.state.wv.us/

Wisconsin
http://www.state.wi.us/

Wyoming
http://www.state.wy.us/

# Entering into a School Setting

Most colleges and universities have an office, usually the Office of Field Experiences, assigned to making student placements for fieldwork. Work through this office to set up your school or classroom visits. Make sure you review whatever guidelines or procedures are available.

When you go to a school to conduct observations, remember that you are visiting the school in a professional role. Wear appropriate clothing. Showing up in a T-shirt that has your favorite band's logo on it may look cool, but it will not impress school staff and teachers with your seriousness. Shorts, tank tops, halter dresses, and similar items are all examples of clothing to avoid wearing.

At the same time, you probably don't need to show up in a suit and tie or a dress. For men, a shirt and/or sweater with nice slacks is fine. For women, slacks and a blouse are fine. Wearing a dress is also acceptable, but make sure it is appropriate in terms of the community.

Some years ago, one of the authors supervised a student teacher who wore a transparent blouse to a field observation at an inner-city middle school. She was extremely upset and offended when the older boys in the school started following her around, making sexually oriented comments. While the boys were behaving in a completely inappropriate way, there would almost certainly not have been a problem if the student observer had been wearing something more subdued.

Another student observer one of us supervised wore torn blue jeans and a T-shirt that featured a well-known beer that proclaimed "Go for the Gusto." While maybe a great outfit for a concert, clothes like this were not appropriate for a high school.

Always be discreet. Don't gossip with students or faculty. Use your common sense. Your ultimate goal is to complete a series of observations and interviews—i.e., to collect information about a social setting. Your job is to blend in, negotiate your way through the observation or interview site, and not be the subject of attention yourself.

Officially, you are a guest at the school you are visiting. You are obligated to follow the rules laid down by the school's administration. It is not your place to discipline a student or to publicly criticize a student, teacher, staff member, or administrator. If you see a problem (students fighting, someone cheating, and so on), report it immediately to an appropriate person. If at all possible, do not get personally involved.

# Setting up a School Observation

If you have to arrange your own observation in a school, do the following:

- Call the school and talk to the principal or the assistant principal. Explain why you want to come to the school.
- Ask for permission to visit both the school and specific sites within the school (a kindergarten class, the library, and so on).

The principal or administrator in charge may want to create a schedule for you. Make sure it includes classroom settings and teacher types that you are interested in. Also make sure you get to see and observe other settings than just classrooms, such as the library, the main office, the cafeteria, and so on. Be sure that you have a chance to informally wander the halls and more public places like playing fields or playgrounds. It is always interesting, for example, to watch the buses as children are arriving or leaving.

When you go to an observation site, it is generally good to check into the office. Many field observation programs have sign-in sheets in either the main office or in the classroom where you are doing your main observations. Often these require the sign-off of a teacher or an administrator.

Many universities and colleges request that students wear an identification tag when they are visiting a school. It is a good idea. If you don't have one, you may want to make one for yourself. It should look something like this:

> MARIA RODRIGUEZ
> Student Observer
> School of Education
> University of Miami

Administrators often place students in observation settings without telling the teachers who are being observed that you are coming. Take a copy of your observation instrument to share with the teacher. This will help the teacher understand the purpose of your visit. Be polite and diplomatic if a teacher is surprised when you appear in his or her class. Teachers do not have to let you observe. You are their guest. If there is a serious problem, ask to be assigned to another setting.

Make clear to the teacher you are assigned to that you are there to observe and not to grade papers, tutor students, or teach a class. Under no circumstances should you be left alone in the classroom with responsibility for the students. This is not your role. If something went seriously wrong, both you and the teacher whom you are observing could be held liable. Once again, if there is a problem, consult the principal or your university supervisor.

# Guidelines for Writing Field Notes

......................................................

**E**ach time you visit a classroom and engage in learning activities with children, you should write field notes afterwards. These field notes are extremely important and should be done carefully and thoughtfully, and be precisely in line with the guidelines presented here in both form and content. As time goes by in your college or university class, your instructor may revise the guidelines, providing more ideas for you to consider and ways to make your field notes clearer.

Your field notes should demonstrate evidence of what you have been learning in the course. The concepts that are introduced and studied in class should gradually become tools that you use increasingly more often and with greater precision in writing your field notes. You should notice growth in your own learning about teaching—especially when you review your field notes at the end of the course and notice how different they are from those at the beginning. In particular, they should reveal new ways you have learned for noticing, thinking about, and analyzing teaching as not only a learning but also social and cultural activity.

Your basic goal in writing field notes is to describe and document everything important that you or another person who is going to work with a child needs to know about the child in order to help him or her learn and develop.

## WRITING DETAILED FIELD NOTES

Field notes need to be as detailed as possible. These procedures should help you:

- As you work with a child, take short, rough notes on a pad or bound notebook to help you remember such things as what the child said or did at key points in an activity; examples of problems, clues, words or reading passages that you and the child encountered; exactly what you said and did at key points in the session to help the child.
- Write up your field notes as soon after the activity as possible, while events are still fresh in your mind.
- Focus on details of the child's behavior and the child's interaction with you, others, and the setting that you think reveal aspects of learning, thinking, and problem-solving strategies.

## ORGANIZATION OF FIELD NOTES

Begin the heading of your field notes with the following information:

Your name:

Name of the school and classroom:

Date: Month/Day/Year

Children: First name of all the children with whom you will be working

Activities: Curriculum area, topic, skill, tasks completed, and level attained

Field notes should be organized into four sections, using these section headings:

    I. GENERAL OBSERVATIONS

    II. NARRATIVE

    III. ANALYSIS AND CONCLUSIONS

    IV. REFLECTION

These are general guidelines. Your instructor may revise these guidelines.

### I. General Observations

This section should provide a general description of the school and the classroom as you found them when you arrived. It should be about a paragraph in length. If some really unusual or surprising event is going on, you may need to write a longer section to fully describe what you see.

### II. Narrative

The narrative should focus on *the behavior of you and the child* (or children) as you interacted throughout the activity—what you actually said and did, as accurately as possible. It should be a running "play-by-play" narrative account of what the child said and did and what you said and did as the activity progressed. You are trying *to show, not to tell*.

What you need to include in a good narrative is everything important that another person who is going to work with the child next needs to know about the child in order to help the child learn and develop. What you *show* in this detailed narrative will be behavior that sheds light on the child's learning, thinking, problem-solving strategies, and other things listed in the "Points to Consider" section.

## III.  Analysis and Conclusions

In this section, you *analyze* the "moving picture" of behavior that you created in the narrative to reach your conclusions regarding important things about the child that you or another person needs to know in order to help the child learn and develop.

The narrative provides evidence for your conclusions. You should explicitly refer back to the behavior, interactions, and events that you described in your narrative. Don't leave it to the reader to make the connections between your narrative and your conclusions. Your conclusions should be about the topics below.

- Where is the child in the activity at present, at what level of performance—how does she or he approach the problems and tasks and think and reason about tasks or problems presented in the activity; what can she or he do alone; what can she or he can do with help, and what kind of help does she or he usually need?

- Has the child made any progress, learned anything, or advanced in any way during the progression of the activity?

- Where should the child go next and what should another person who works with the child next work on with him or her? EXACTLY what is just beyond the child's ability to do alone, but near enough to where she or he is now that she or he can learn with the guided assistance of an adult?

### *Points to Consider*

You should point out the things that seem most important to discuss in relation to the activity you are observing—the ones that were most influential for the progress you and the child made and that might be of particular importance for you or another intern or teacher who is going to work with the child.

Obviously, some of the points to consider are interrelated. You can weave a subset of interrelated issues together and discuss them. It is important for you to remember that for every point you consider, you should always end your discussion with where the child is and where the child can go next in the activity.

- What (if any) change, progress, learning, did the child demonstrate during the activity? Be sure your narrative describes the child's behavior *before* and *after* these changes. What makes you think these are important? Where does this mean the child should go in the next activity?

- What does the child's performance indicate about where she or he is in the activity? How has she or he progressed in the activity? Where does she or he need to go next?

- What exactly did the child seem to know about the activity, thinking processes, and learning strategies necessary for performing the activity successfully? What exactly did the child not seem to know or be aware of? What behavior indicated this? At what level of performance in the activity is the child that he or she was not at before? Where does this mean the child should go next in the activity?

- What strategies, techniques, and ways of thinking did the child actually use during the activity? How was she or he thinking about the activity and the tasks included within it? What behaviors suggest this? What do the strategies, techniques, and ways of thinking that the child was using suggest about where she or he is, how she or he progressed, and where she or he needs to go next in the activity?

- Where do you think the child learned these strategies and ways of thinking? What does this suggest about where the child is and where she or he needs to go next in the activity?

- What kinds of problems did the child encounter during the activity? What does this suggest about where the child is and where she or he needs to go next in the activity?

- What did the child do when she or he needed help or encountered problems completing the activity (give example)? What does this indicate about where she or he is, how she or he is progressing, and where she or he needs to go next in the activity?

- What was the child's level of expertise in using materials, such as books, manuals, computers, crayons, scissors, in the activity? What does this suggest about how to explain where she or he is in the activity, how she or he is progressing, and where she or he needs to go next?

- Did the child's behavior toward the materials change at any point during the activity? If so, exactly when and in what ways? What was going on when this change occurred? Can you make any guesses about what might have brought about the change? What does this tell you about the child that might be useful to another adult who works with him or her now or in the future?

- What kind of experience was this activity for you? Did you understand the activity and the materials to be used? Did you understand how to use the materials? Did you understand the instructional strategies? How do you think your level of understanding of materials and instructional strategies affected the child's experience and performance?

## IV.  Reflection

- What things did you learn about children, how they learn, and how they develop?

- What things did you learn about teaching, subject matter, skills, and materials?

- What things did you learn about how children interact with their peers and adults?

- What things did you learn about individual differences (interest, motivation, prior knowledge, etc.) among children?

- What was a big surprise, great success, or disappointment for you in this activity?

- What questions do you have about your experience that you would like discussed in your class?

- What exactly did the child seem to know about the activity, thinking processes, and learning strategies necessary for performing the activity successfully? What exactly did the child not seem to know or be aware of? What behavior indicated this? At what level of performance in the activity is the child that he or she was not at before? Where does this mean the child should go next in the activity?

- What, if any, kinds of problems did the child encounter during the activity? Provide details about the main ones. What does this suggest about where the child is and where she or he needs to go next in the activity?

- What did the child do when she or he needed help or encountered difficulty completing the activity? What is (are) example(s) that demonstrate this? What does this indicate about where she or he is, how she or he is progressing, and where she or he needs to go next in the activity?

- What was your own experience with the activity? Did you understand the activity? What strategies worked well? How might this have affected the child's experience and performance?

# Participant Observation Field Notes

Among the most powerful research tools of anthropologists and sociologists is *participant observation*. As a participant observer, you take notes and observe what it is that you are doing. To some extent, participant observation can be thought of as a self-monitoring process in which you carefully observe and collect data on your personal activities.

At some point either in your fieldwork or in your beginning teaching, you will start working with students. This does not mean that you stop doing fieldwork. What you will do is become a participant observer.

The purpose for writing field notes of your participation in teaching and related activities is threefold: First, field notes help beginning teachers to focus their attention on the issues of how children learn, what they learn, and how they use what they already know in the context of school activities. In doing so, you should look for instances of topics, content, events, and issues read about and discussed in your college and university courses that are related to events in the teaching and learning activity in which you participate.

The second purpose for writing field notes as a participant observer is to provide you and the classroom teacher you are working with, and/or your course instructor and classmates in your university or college classes, with information about aspects of an activity that may not leave any other record except by your written summary as an observer. For example, create a record of the peer interactions of a group of first graders in negotiating who gets to read first, answer a question first, or use the computer first, or who seems to get his or her way. This kind of information may only be available if you conduct systematic observations and summaries.

While the classroom record-keeping system of the teacher you are working with or that you are keeping yourself as part of a grade book or evaluation system will probably provide a summary of activities, tasks, and skills children have completed and their level of success, this information will probably be incomplete. Your participant observation notes can provide more complete information about how children respond in the activity and their interactions with other children and interns. For example, did a child only respond in an activity if you prodded, suggested answers, or gave hints during the activity? As beginning teachers working with children in learning activities, you should help children when they need it, but give only as much help as they need. When you do intervene, it is important to record how, why, what happened, and why you think it helped or did not help the child.

Third, as participant observers, you need to reflect on each activity in which you engage and include your reflections in your field notes. Reviewing, thinking, and writing about experiences helps you as an observer formulate what has been experienced, interpret its meaning, and communicate it to others. Successful teachers do this after lessons and at the end of the school day. At the end of the day they also review and interpret critical events that occurred in their classrooms during the day. Keeping diaries and journals is a requirement of field experiences and student teaching. They are also valuable tools master teachers regularly use as part of their work. Developing the habit of reflection now will make the process even more meaningful for you as you move from taking part in field experiences to student teaching and on to professional teaching.

# Journals and Diaries

The tradition of keeping personal journals and diaries is old and honorable. It is one of the best ways to keep information organized about a specific observational setting like a classroom or school. Among the greatest diaries in literature is the one written by Samual Pepys (1633-1703). Pepys's *Diary* is still read today because of its extraordinary detail, the quality of its language, and the historical interest of its topics. Look at the following excerpt for December 21, 1663, where Pepys describes a cock fight in which roosters with small sharpened knives or "spurs" attached to their feet are allowed to fight one another to the death.

> . . . took Coach, and being directed by sight of bills upon the walls, did goe to Shooe lane to see a Cocke-fighting at a new pit there—a sport I was never at in my life. But Lord, to see the strange variety of people, from Parliament-man . . . to the poorest prentices, bakers, brewers, butchers, draymen, and what not; and all this fellows one with another in swearing, cursing and betting. I soon had enough of it; and yet I would not but have seen it once, it being strange to observe the nature of those poor creatures, how they will fight until they drop down dead upon the table and strike after they are ready to give up the ghost—not offering to run way when they are weary or wounded past doing further. . . . One thing more it is strange to see, how people of this poor rank, that look as if they had not bread to put in their mouths, shall bet 3 or 4l at one bet and lose it, and yet bet as much the next battell, as they call every make of two cocks—so that one of them will lose 10 or 20l at a meeting.

While the language is archaic and difficult to read, it is also vivid and literate. Pepys keeps our interest by describing what he saw in great detail. In doing so, he leaves a record of a world we would otherwise not know about.

Keeping a research journal or diary is essential to doing field observations. You may not create a literary masterpiece like Pepys's diary, but even a fairly modest observation diary can be an interesting and important record of what goes on in a classroom or school.

Your diary is where you take your field notes and keep a record of all you have observed. It allows you to come back and see how things have changed or remained the same in a particular school or setting.

You can note specific quotes or comments. It is a place where you can reflect or speculate on what it is that you are observing.

Some suggestions that you may find helpful in keeping an effective observational journal:

- Use a bound notebook. Do not pull pages out of it to do other things. Field notes taken on scraps of paper get lost or misfiled.
- Date every one of your entries. You may even want to include the time of day.
- Write in pen, not in pencil. Do not erase materials or entries; simply cross them through if you want to delete something.
- Always carry your journal with you. Do not leave it somewhere that it can be found or stolen.
- Do not share the content of your journal with individuals at your observation site. Your journal is a personal document. Think of it as being like a private diary. Its content could be potentially damaging to others. Do you really want to have a teacher you have been observing read a comment like: "The teacher seems poorly prepared and short tempered with most of the children. She clearly has favorites and tends to work with selected boys, while ignoring both the boys and the girls who are ethnically and racially different from herself." While the teacher may need to hear this, it is not your place as a visitor to the school to criticize her. Your job is to observe, collect data, and understand how schools work and function.

You can share your observations and the content of your journal with other people for professional purposes (fellow students, your professors, and so on), but you should be discreet and professional in doing so—most important, NEVER identify the teacher or children by name.

Be as detailed as possible. Describe the setting and atmosphere, as well as what actually occurs there. You can never provide enough detail.

*Note: Although we provide observation forms for you throughout this book, we would like to suggest that keeping all of your notes in a journal will help you keep your work organized. You may want to copy the forms by hand into your journal, or copy them and paste them in appropriate sections.

# Creating a Journal or Diary

**T**he following section is intended to provide you with general guidelines for keeping a journal or diary of your field experiences for your university or college courses, community settings, school activities, classroom activities, and your participation as tutor, teacher assistant, and other field experiences.

Begin your journal or diary by identifying the date, place, time, and kind of activity, followed by both the purpose of the assigned activity and your own purpose. Then enter the events that make an impression on you, along with your comments about the events.

## KINDS OF COMMENTS TO PUT IN YOUR JOURNAL OR DIARY

1. Comments relating your experiences to previous educational experiences.
   - K–12 experiences
   - College or university
   - Informal teaching experience in community institutions
2. Comments relating your experiences to college or university courses.
   - Class discussions
   - Textbook content
   - Content of assigned readings
   - Content of videos observed
   - Observation performed in schools and other field experiences
3. Comments about planning.
   - Plans based on observations of pupils
   - Reflections about your confidences or uneasiness
   - Reflections about what and how you are learning
4. Comments about tutoring and teaching small groups.
   - What changes would you make in your teaching plan if you were teaching the lesson again?
   - What revisions would solve the problems you encountered?
5. Comments about critical incidents.
   - What was unexpected?
   - What intrigued you?

- What questions did you ponder?

6. Comments about successful experiences.
   - What pleased you?
   - What worked well?
   - What evidence was there of success?

7. Comments about problems you encountered.
   - What do you find to be frustrating?
   - What do you find to be persistent problems?
   - Describe your disappointments

8. Comments about professional relationships.
   - With whom and why do you share your success?
   - Comments about parents
   - What do parents want to know about the school and their children?
   - Problems you have communicating with parents
   - How do parents communicate with you?
   - Do parents understand the classroom curriculum?
   - Do parents understand classroom rules?

9. Comments and reflection on critical incidents. If you are observing or participating in a classroom, you may observe or be part of a critical incident. A critical incident is an event or disruption in the classroom during your classroom teaching or during other professional interactions that has a significant effect on your instruction, or your feelings toward teaching, colleagues, or administrators.
   - What was the critical incident?
   - What was happening when the event occurred?
   - What action did you or others take as a result of the incident that you found to be helpful to your understanding of professional practice?
   - What action taken by you or others as a result the incident did you think was confusing or in contradiction with what you believed was appropriate practice?
   - What were the most important questions you asked yourself about the critical incident? Have your beliefs or values remained the same or are they changing?
   - How can you connect this experience to a specific undergraduate course or another field experience?

10. Comments and reflection on teaching practices and certification standards. Take a moment to think about the teaching practices or certification standards you have to meet to become a teacher. You might be wondering how you are going to master and understand all of them at this time in your career. Why don't you sort them into categories such as "easy," "difficult but doable," and "definitely need help."

    - Which of the practices or standards is affected by this observation or participation activity? Why?

    - Which of the practices or standards do you think you need to give more attention and study to? How do you know? How did your observation or participation activity influence you?

    - Which of the practices do think you are performing fairly well as a result of your observation or participation activity? How do you know? How did your observation or participation activity influence you?

    - As a result of you observation or participation activity, what plans do you have for improving those that you identified as "easy," "difficult but doable," "definitely need help"?

    - If your teacher education program requires that you develop and present a professional folio to demonstrate the attainment of practices and standards, what material from this observation or participation experience can you include?

    - Comments about future professional development plans.

As a result of this observation or participation activity, what knowledge, concept, or skill have you identified that you need to learn more about? What learning materials and activities might be helpful? How will you know you are learning what you need to learn?

# Writing and Reflection

W e don't learn and develop from experiences as much as we learn from reflecting on information and experiences. Reflection is the process of constructing meaning and knowledge by thinking about and interpreting the results of goal-oriented activity in which you have engaged. Reflection is the hallmark of professional practice.

Learning to reflect on your professional activities will help you to become a reflective practitioner who can select from a menu of alternatives that are in the best interest of your students and your professional development, as opposed to a procedural professional whose professional actions are determined by context. Reflective practice begins with "doing" observations of schools and classroom activities, such as teaching and learning, returning to the events observed, selecting those events that stood out for you, and thinking about them and what they mean. This kind of reflection will enable you to learn to convert information you obtain and experience you have into professional knowledge and personal understanding about teaching.

Since you have already clocked at least twelve years in schools, you probably feel like you already know quite a bit about the culture of schooling, curriculum, teaching, learners, materials, and the like. As noted earlier, your previous experience can be an impediment to learning how to teach. Observing and participating in schools and reflecting on your experience will help you confront some of your misconceptions. You will be able to both connect course content to real classroom situations and to identify events that need further elaboration in your course. By writing in your journal, you will be able to identify issues and activities that are unsettling for you and formulate and communicate your thoughts to yourself and others. You will also be able to identify what you know and don't know and what is still confusing for you.

Journals and diaries are tools to assist you record and transform your assumptions and ideas about teaching, learning, human development, and learning to teach into personal understanding. They provide you the means to analyze, describe, feel, express, and question your understandings, frustrations, and developments as a prospective teacher. They are a place where you can write down sentences, paragraphs, ideas, feelings, questions, and reactions to critical classroom events, pupil response to instruction, and conversations with pupils and colleagues. Writing in a journal will help you complete your thoughts as you deliberate about your observations and reactions to teaching and learning issues, with the intention of connecting them to your previous experiences in K–12 schools and teacher preparation course work. A journal is also a place in which to write entries about content discussed in class, course readings, observations, tutoring experience, or reflections about university course activities. It is a place to jot down your thoughts to prepare for class. Over time, you can revisit your written records, think back on your experiences, and deliberate on what your have learned, index it to classroom events, and transform your knowledge about teaching. By keeping a journal or diary, you will be taking steps to master a tool for analysis and reflection and will be incorporating it into your teaching activity and professional development plans.

# Ethical Issues

.......................

*"Loose lips sink ships."*

—a traditional saying in the U.S. Navy

Anyone who conducts fieldwork must consider ethical issues involved in research. When you enter the field to collect data, you are asking for the trust of the people whom you are interviewing and observing. This means that you cannot use the information that you have collected inappropriately.

What are some examples of the type of ethical issues that can come up as you conduct your work as a classroom observer and interviewer? Some years ago, one of the authors had a student who had been doing observations in a local school in Miami, Florida. Over Christmas break she returned to her home in New Jersey, over a thousand miles from where she had conducted her observations. While out to dinner with her parents and friends, she discussed the school and teacher she had been observing. Her comments made fun of the teacher whom she was working with and were highly unprofessional and unfair. Unbeknownst to her, the principal from the school she was observing was seated at the table next to her. He heard everything she said.

The principal said nothing, but when the new semester began, he contacted the university and asked that the student not be allowed to come back to his school. He explained that he felt that her behavior at the restaurant had been highly unprofessional and that the teacher she was making fun of was one of the very best people working in his school. When the student found out that she was being removed from the school, she was shocked and extremely upset. She explained that she actually liked the teacher and the work she was doing and was joking about her just for fun with her parents and friends.

There are a number of issues at work in this story. The first and most important is the ethical issue. It involves keeping your observations in the field confidential. In your fieldwork, you are describing things that can have a very real impact on people if they are made public. Information that you report can often be misunderstood, causing problems as well. Discretion is key in doing fieldwork. Doing the ethical thing and protecting your subjects and the information that they provide you as a researcher will also protect you. You cannot get into trouble for something you have not shared or said.

You need to be very careful in keeping your field notes. First, don't let them out of your sight. You do not want them to be seen by people for whom they are not intended. Imagine the embarrassment for everyone if someone showed your observations of a particular student or teacher to other people. Using a code name is often a good idea. Rename the school you are doing your observations in. Make sure it is not the name of another school in the district. Likewise, use coded names for teachers, students, and classes you are observing.

Do not share your observations with other people, unless you have a professional reason for doing so. This does not mean you cannot mention your observations to a friend, or perhaps your roommate, but you must do so discreetly. Keeping materials confidential does not mean that you cannot share them in a public setting like a university class, but once again, you need to be discreet. Only discuss those things you need to and always keep in mind that you need to protect the rights of those whom you are observing.

The question may arise as to what you should do if you see something that is illegal happen while you are in the school. This can be a very difficult issue. If you see a student in a high school selling drugs, for example, it probably is not a good idea to immediately turn that person in. You probably should withdraw from the situation being observed and discreetly bring up what you have seen with your college or university supervisor, or possibly with the school's administration. Sometimes making the right decision may be difficult. If you see something like a student's being beaten up in a hallway, once again, try to find help. But unless absolutely necessary, do not try to break things up by yourself.

Ethical behavior, to a large degree, involves using your common sense. Remember, it is your obligation to protect the rights of those whom you are studying. In medicine, doctors follow the ancient Hippocratic oath of essentially "doing no unnecessary harm." Just as a doctor or nurse should do no harm in practicing medicine, you should do no harm to your subjects as you are observing and interviewing them.

Research subjects are not to be exploited for your advantage. If a person does not wish to answer a question you are asking in an interview, you do not have the right to insist that they give you a response. It is their right to refuse to give you information in the form of an interview or as part of an observation. As a researcher you are always obliged to respect the rights and privacy of the people whom you are studying.

Finally, be aware that you need to professionally keep a distance from the students and even the teachers you are observing. It is not appropriate, and may even be ethically compromising, for you to ask a student in a classroom or school where you are observing out for a date. This may be more of a problem than you realize. Perhaps you are a freshman or sophomore in college conducting observations at a local high school. It is very possible that you are attracted to a junior or senior student in your observational setting. There may only be a year or two apart between you in age. The student may look up to you as an outsider and as an older college student.

The fact is, that as an observer you have a professional role to fulfill. Dating a student represents a potential conflict of interest that can have ethical implications in terms of your behavior. You don't need to learn the intimate details of the private lives of the students you are observing. Likewise, the students you are observing do not need to know about your private life.

The ethical rules that apply to dealing with students to a large degree also apply in terms of the teachers you are observing. Keeping a professional distance is extremely important as an observer. Besides being the right thing to do, it will help you prepare for how you should behave when you actually become a teacher.

# Conclusion

So, you have been introduced to the basics of doing fieldwork. Now you have a bit of theory under your belt, as well as some practical tips about how to go into the field. Part II of this book provides you with observation and interview schedules you can use in the field. These schedules are intended to be used in a wide range of settings. They are starting points and can be added to or modified, depending on your needs.

Keep in mind that fieldwork involves a constant process of adaptation and reflection. Go out and see what you can learn by observing, listening, viewing, and participating. You should find what you do not only interesting, but also invaluable to you in becoming a more skilled and productive teacher and border crosser.

# PART II

........................

# Observation Instruments

**P**art I of this book provided a brief overview of issues and methods for conducting field observations and interviews in school settings. Part II provides observation schedules to use in your fieldwork.

These observation schedules do not need to be followed slavishly; instead, use them as you see fit. Adapt and modify them in ways that work best for your work in the field.

## General Observation of a Classroom

School (Use a Code): _____     Observer: _____

Grade: _____     Date: _____

Curriculum Area: _____     Time In: _____     Time Out: _____

*Directions:* During this activity, you will be observing a general classroom setting. Write as many observations as you possibly can in the space provided below. Then answer the questions included on the summary observation sheet.

## Summary of Observation

General Observation of a Classroom

School (Use a Code):            Observer:

Grade:                           Date:

*Directions:* Summarize what you have found out about the teacher you have observed and the routines he or she follows in his or her work.

What did you observe that you expected to see?

What did you observe that was unexpected?

What was the most important event or behavior you observed?

What key point about your observation would you like to stress in class?

What is the most important question raised by your observation?

# Looking for Root Metaphors in the Classroom

Root metaphors are images or metaphors that are deeply embedded in a culture or society. In Western culture important root metaphors include the concept of the universe functioning as a machine, the idea that the United States is the defender of democracy throughout the world, and the idea that the world is focused around everything that is human.

Often root metaphors are simply taken for granted and assumed to be correct—or that they simply describe the world as it is. Root metaphors often reflect specific biases. The myth of White superiority that dominated so much of nineteenth- and twentieth-century educational thought would be an example of a root metaphor.

Go into a classroom setting. Try to detect root metaphors at work in the teacher's instruction and student discussions. Look in science and social studies textbooks to see if you can find examples of root metaphors at work. Use the form below to list at least three root metaphors you have discovered. Write a paragraph about the meaning of each and why you think it might be important.

Metaphor:

Description:




Metaphor:

Description




Metaphor:

Description

# Observing an Individual Student

School (Use a Code): _____     Observer: _____

Grade: _____     Date: _____

Curriculum Area: _____     Time In: _____     Time Out: _____

*Directions:* Use the following schedule to observe an individual student and his or her characteristics and activities in class. Use the space on the right-hand side of the page to make notes about what you observe.

| Kind of Behavior | Brief Description of Student |
| --- | --- |
| On Task | |
| On Wrong Task | |
| Out of Seat | |
| Talking | |

Playing

Daydreaming

Disruptive Behavior

Other (Describe)

## Summary of Observation

Observing an Individual Student

School (Use a Code): _____ Observer: _____

Grade: _____ Date: _____

Summarize your observation:




What did you observe that you expected to see?




What did you observe that was unexpected?




What was the most important event or behavior you observed?




What is the most important question raised by your observation?

# Student Interaction in the Classroom

School (Use a Code): _____     Observer: _____

Grade: _____     Date: _____

Curriculum Area: _____     Time In: _____     Time Out: _____

*Directions:* In this observation module you will observe students interacting in a classroom. Be as unobtrusive as possible in the classroom before any students arrive. Jot down notes as they begin to arrive. Summarize your observations in the spaces provided below. Some suggestions for your notes are as follows:

Notice who arrives first and last.

How many and what age and gender are the students in this class?

Do students remain in the same groups inside the classroom as those in which they arrived?

Look at the overall spacing between groups. Is it uniform? Does it reflect furniture or resource location or friendship groups? Are there any cliques?

Who are the isolates?

How much movement between groups occurs? Note how changes in groupings occur during the class period.

What roles do particular students play? For example, who is the joker, the cynic, the teacher's pet, the introvert, etc.?

Which students raise their hands most often and least often (or never) when the teacher asks a question?

Which students does the teacher never call on?

Is the behavior of the students who sit in the back of the room different from that of the rest of the class?

Which students seem to be paying most and least attention and what is the range of attention spans?

Which students ask for help and whom do they ask (the teacher, nearby students)?

Which students receive the most praise and which receive the most criticism? Which students seem to be ignored?

Try to determine the extent of any division of labor in the class or within the groups. Are there different roles? Do all students carry out the same tasks? Are roles and tasks fixed or do they shift among students? Who seems to assign these roles or tasks? How smooth running and cohesive is the class and is each group?

If there are groups, how much communication and sharing exist among them?

Is the relationship among students mostly cooperative, competitive, or individualistic? For example, when the teacher asks a student a question, do other students help the first student answer it, or do they try to answer it themselves?

On which students does the teacher rely to help decide when to move on? When teachers decide to move on to another activity or topic, they commonly base this decision on their judgment that certain students have "gotten" the material.

## Summary of Observation

Student Interaction in the Classroom

School (Use a Code): _____    Observer: _____

Grade: _____    Date: _____

Summarize and describe your observation.

## Impressions of Student Characteristics

| School (Use a Code): | Observer: | |
|---|---|---|
| Grade: | Date: | |
| Curriculum Area: | Time In: | Time Out: |

*Directions:* Observe some students. The cafeteria during lunch and the playground or school grounds during recess are possible places, as well as when students enter or leave class. Record your observations on the sheet provided. Some possible characteristics to notice might be:

Dress. How are the students dressed? Comment on neatness and apparent affluence. Note differences in dress among groups of students.

Language. What is their out-of-class language like? How is it different from their in-class language? What sorts of emotions do they express with their language? Do they use abusive language?

Interests. If you are unobtrusive, you will be able to overhear fragments of conversations. What do the students talk about? Teachers? Sports and cars? Grades? The opposite sex? Clothes? Current events? Tests? Note differences in topics of conversations for different groups.

Groups. What groups can you identify? (Groups are particularly noticeable in secondary schools.) Some groups you might notice are "jocks," "druggies," "straights," "punks," "nerds," "preppies," and students of various racial or ethnic backgrounds. How would you characterize each group? Consider their dress, language, interests and so on. How rigid is group definition? That is, are some students members of more than one group? Or, do some members of groups mix with members of other groups? Are there loners? What are their characteristics?

Territory. Does each of the groups have its own territory? Which one has the most territory? The least territory? How closely guarded is each group's territory?

Conflict. What sorts of conflict do you observe? Are the protagonists members of different groups? What is the source of the conflict (e.g., physical or verbal abuse, invasion of one group's territory by another)? How is the conflict settled (if at all) and by whom?

Dominance and Power. Do any of the groups appear to be dominant? Which are the most and the least powerful groups? What is the source of each group's power (e.g., academic skills, athletic skill, muscle, "street knowledge")? Do any of the groups depend on adult approval for their power?

# Summary of Observation

Impressions of Student Characteristics

School (Use a Code): _____    Observer: _____

Grade: _____    Date: _____

*Directions:* Summarize your impressions of the characteristics of the students you have observed. Who are they and what is it like to "live" in this school?

Setting:

Description of students:

# Observing a Child with a Learning or Behavior Problem

School (Use a Code): _____   Observer: _____

Grade: _____   Date: _____

Curriculum Area: _____   Time In: _____   Time Out: _____

*Directions:* Select a child who you think might have a learning or behavior problem. Observe him or her for 30 minutes. Record behaviors such as the number of times he or she requests help and how he or she participates in different activities. Record on-task behavior and teacher interaction. Use an additional page to add other categories you think are important.

Brief Description of Student:

Times Needing Help (Check):

|  |  |  |  |  |  |  |  |  |  |
|---|---|---|---|---|---|---|---|---|---|
|  |  |  |  |  |  |  |  |  |  |
|  |  |  |  |  |  |  |  |  |  |
|  |  |  |  |  |  |  |  |  |  |

Ways Student Participates in Activities:

Behavior on Task:

Interaction with Teacher:

## Summary of Observation

Observing a Child with a Learning or Behavior Problem

School (Use a Code):                     Observer:

Grade:                                   Date:

Summarize what you have found out about the student you have observed.

# Observing a Child Who Is Exceptionally Bright or Creative

School (Use a Code): _____     Observer: _____

Grade: _____     Date: _____

Curriculum Area: _____     Time In: _____     Time Out: _____

*Directions:* Select a child who you think is exceptionally bright or creative. Observe him or her for 30 minutes. Record behaviors such as the number of times he or she requests help and how he or she participates in different activities. Record on-task behavior and teacher interaction. Use an additional page to add other categories you think are important.

Brief Description of Student:



Times Needing Help (Check):

|  |  |  |  |  |  |  |  |  |  |
|--|--|--|--|--|--|--|--|--|--|
|  |  |  |  |  |  |  |  |  |  |
|  |  |  |  |  |  |  |  |  |  |

Ways Student Participates in Activities:



Behavior on Task:



Interaction with Teacher:

## Summary of Observation

Observing a Child Who Is Exceptionally Bright or Creative

School (Use a Code): _____    Observer: _____

Grade: _____    Date: _____

Summarize what you have found out about the student you have observed.

# Learning about Teachers' Routines

School (Use a Code): _____ Observer: _____

Grade: _____ Date: _____

Curriculum Area: _____ Time In: _____ Time Out: _____

*Directions:* Use the form below to conduct an observation of a teacher's routine.

| Things to Observe | Description of Routine Procedures Observed |
|---|---|
| Areas of Management and Organization | |
| Providing Activity for Early Arriving Students | |
| Beginning School Day | |
| Directing Teacher Aide or Volunteer | |
| Organizing and Providing Seatwork | |

| Things to Observe | Description of Routine Procedures Observed |
|---|---|
| Making Homework Assignments | |
| Checking Assignments | |
| Reviewing Assignments | |
| Convening Students into a Group | |
| Reconvening Group to Class | |
| Holding Student Conferences | |

## Summary of Observation

Learning about Teachers' Routines

School (Use a Code):           Observer:

Grade:           Date:

Summarize what you have found out about the teacher you have observed and the routines he or she follows in his or her work.

# Phases of Instruction

School (Use a Code): _____    Observer: _____

Grade: _____    Date: _____

Curriculum Area: _____    Time In: _____  Time Out: _____

*Directions:* Use the form below to conduct an observation of the phases of instruction found in a classroom.

| Lesson Phase | Teacher | Description of Activity | Student(s) Responses |
|---|---|---|---|
| Pre-Lesson | | | |
| During Lesson | | | |
| Post-Lesson | | | |

# Summary of Observation

Phases of Instruction

School (Use a Code):              Observer:

Grade:                            Date:

*Directions:* Use the form below to summarize your observations on the effectiveness of the teacher whom you observed.

What did you observe that you expected to see?




What did you observe that was unexpected?




What was the most important event or behavior you observed?




What key point about your observation would you like to stress in class?




What is the most important question raised by your observation?

## Observing Language Arts Instruction

School (Use a Code):          Observer:

Grade:          Date:

Time In:          Time Out:

*Directions:* Use this form to conduct an observation of the teaching of language arts in a classroom setting.

Make a rough sketch of the classroom you are observing in this space:

Instructional Activities and Tasks Presented to Students

1. Describe the instructional activity. For example, was it a listening, viewing, hands-on, interactive, or writing activity?

2. Describe the purpose of the activity and describe how you determined the purpose.

3. Did the students know the purpose of the activity? What evidence did you observe that suggested the students knew the purpose of the activity?

4. What kinds of instructional strategies did the teacher use to engage the children in the activity? Circle or check appropriate bullet(s).

   • Teacher invited students to answer questions and evaluated their answers.
   • Teacher invited students to answer questions and followed up on their answers with more conversation.
   • Teacher asked students to recall information they probably knew before the lesson began.
   • Teacher asked students questions based on what they viewed, heard, or wrote.
   • Teacher asked the students questions and gave them time to think about the answers.
   • Teacher asked students to make oral or written predictions and then engaged them in discussion about whether their predictions were confirmed or disconfirmed.
   • Teacher asked students to freely discuss their responses to material listened to or viewed.

- Teacher engaged the students in discussing the kind of material they listened to or read—for example, fiction, drama, poetry, historical fiction, or information text.
- The teacher engaged the students in discussing the ideas, opinions, and interpretations of others to the material.

Other (please explain):

---

5. Take one of the activities you selected above and describe what was said and how it was said.

---

6. How did the teacher give students feedback? Circle or check appropriate bullet(s).

- Teacher did not give feedback.
- Teacher provided students with mostly evaluative feedback, indicating whether they were right or wrong.
- Teacher elaborated on the responses of students with more explanation and invited other students to provide explanations.
- Teacher followed up on student responses, inviting them to ponder open-ended questions or explain their answers, whether correct or incorrect, to others.

Other (please explain):

---

7. Take one instance of how feedback was provided by the teacher and describe what was said and how it was said.

---

8. To what extent did the teacher facilitate discussion among students? Circle or check appropriate bullet(s).

   • There was very little discussion among students.
   • Discussion reflected very little knowledge of content.
   • Discussion was mainly about how to follow directions and get answers.
   • Students frequently asked each other to elaborate on their contributions to the discussion.
   • Students frequently asked each other to take a different point of view.

9. Take one instance of the teacher's encouraging discussion among the students and describe it.



10. To what extent do you think the students were actively engaged in the activity? Circle or check bullet(s).

    • Actively engaged
    • Somewhat engaged
    • Passively disengaged (e.g., students appeared lethargic and were rarely on task)
    • Not engaged at all

11. Provide a brief description of the kinds of student behavior on which you decided how the students were engaged.



12. What were your overall impressions of the lesson? Circle or check appropriate bullet(s).

    • Lesson was too difficult the children.
    • Lesson was too easy for the children.
    • Lesson was about the right level of difficulty.
    • Most of the children understood the lesson and learned subject matter or skills.
    • Some children would probably benefit with more instruction on the topic.
    • Some children would probably benefit from some independent work on the topic.

## Summary of Observation

Observing Language Arts Instruction

School (Use a Code): _____  Observer: _____

Grade: _____  Date: _____

Summarize what you have observed.

# Observing Discussion of Text Read

School (Use a Code): _____   Observer: _____

Grade: _____   Date: _____

Time In: _____   Time Out: _____

1. Briefly describe the lesson (listening or writing) as presented either orally or in writing by the teacher. Use the teacher's language in your description.

2. During this lesson, the teacher mostly asked questions designed to get students to (you may select more than one):

   - Teacher did not ask questions.
   - Recall literal information.
   - Make oral or written predictions.
   - Articulate ideas and opinions about material.
   - Articulate their response or feelings to text.
   - Identify the writing genre (e.g., fiction, historical fiction, etc.).
   - Critique and respond to each other's ideas and interpretations.
   - Apply what was read or heard to different situation.

   Provide EVIDENCE using verbatim accounts of the discourse in the classroom:

3. The teacher's feedback to students' responses was (you may mark more than one item):

- No feedback provided.
- All responses accepted regardless of their correctness/or plausibility.
- Responses evaluated only for correctness or plausibility by the teacher (e.g., right or wrong).
- Teacher explained or elaborated on the correctness of the response.
- Teacher explored student thinking, knowledge, and understanding correct response through additional questioning.
- Teacher pressed students to defend or justify responses.
- Teacher explored student thinking, knowledge, and understanding of incorrect/plausible responses.
- Teachers used questions to provide clues or to prompt further thinking.

Provide EVIDENCE using verbatim accounts of the discourse in the classroom:

4. To what extent did student exchanges with peers reflect substantive conversation about ideas?

- There were no exchanges among peers.
- Students' exchanges with peers reflected little or no substantive conversations about literacy.
- Most students only asked one another for a clarification of directions given by the teacher or simply accepted someone's answer without an explanation of how it was found.
- Students never asked classmates for a clarification of an answer or to defend and justify their answers.
- Students asked their classmates to justify or defend an answer or interpretation and/or questioned the correctness of some answers.

Provide EVIDENCE using verbatim accounts of the discourse in the classroom:

5. During the lesson:

- Students rarely asked any questions.
- Students asked questions that were irrelevant to the material.
- Students asked questions that were mostly procedural, such as to clarify directions.
- Students asked questions that were seeking to find /discover /clarify the "correct" answers.
- Students asked questions that pressed peers to justify their ideas or that questioned the legitimacy of peers' ideas.

Provide EVIDENCE using verbatim accounts of the discourse in the classroom:

6. During this lesson most students (75% plus) most of the time (75% plus) appeared to be:

- Highly engaged with the academic content.
- Engaged with the academic content.
- Somewhat engaged with the academic content.
- Weakly engaged with the academic content.
- Passively disengaged (e.g., students appeared lethargic and were rarely on lesson).
- Actively disengaged (e.g., students were rarely on lesson and many were disrupting the lesson).

Add any comments or information that you think would be of interest in describing the lesson you observed.

## Summary of Observation

Observing Discussion of Text Read

School (Use a Code):

Observer:                                Date:

Summarize what you have learned from your observation.

# Observing Reading Skills Instruction

School (Use a Code):        Observer:

Grade:        Date:

Time In:        Time Out:

**1.0 Using Diagnostic Data:** This observation includes everything the teacher does, indicating that instruction is based on previous or concurrent diagnosis. Thus, if the teacher checks diagnostic data or other information to select students for instruction or to select instructional activities, collects diagnostic data, or makes diagnostic notes, use this category.

| Observed | Not Observed | |
|---|---|---|
| | | **1.1 Checks diagnostic data:** The teacher checks diagnostic data or other information to select students for instruction or to select instructional activities. |
| | | **1.2 Collects diagnostic data:** The teacher collects diagnostic data to select students for instruction or to select instructional activities. |
| | | **1.3 Makes diagnostic notes:** The teacher makes diagnostic notes. |

**2.0 Teaching Reading Skills:** This category includes what a teacher does to instruct students on reading skills.

| Observed | Not Observed | |
|---|---|---|
| | | **2.1 Provides explanation for rule, skill, or strategy:** The teacher names, defines, explains, and/or gives students information on the relevance of a rule, skill, or strategy. |
| | | **2.2 Asks for student translation:** The teacher asks students to repeat (usually in their own words) how to use or perform the rule, skill, or strategy. |
| | | **2.3 Models rule, skill, or strategy:** The teacher models or demonstrates (shows and thinks aloud) how to use or perform the rule, skill, or strategy. |

| Observed | Not Observed | |
|----------|--------------|---|
| | | **2.4 Asks students to perform the rule, skill, or strategy:** The teacher asks students to complete an example requiring use of the rule, skill, or strategy to determine their level of understanding before assigning practice. |

**3.0 Providing Guided Practice and Application:** This category includes what a teacher does to provide students with practice on a rule, skill, or strategy and what the teacher does to enable students to apply a rule, skill, or strategy.

| Observed | Not Observed | |
|----------|--------------|---|
| | | **3.1 Assigns isolated practice (worksheets):** The teacher assigns students practice with worksheets or similar material. |
| | | **3.2 Assigns contextual practice (reading material):** The teacher assigns students practice in material such as basal selections and other reading material. |
| | | **3.3 Helps with practice:** The teacher helps students with problems related to practicing the rule, skill, or strategy. |
| | | **3.4 Reviews rule, skill, or strategy:** The teacher reviews previous instruction on the rule, skill, or strategy during practice or before or during application. |
| | | **3.5 Assigns application in supplementary material:** The teacher assigns application of a rule, skill, or strategy in supplementary reading materials such as collections of stories accompanying published programs. |
| | | **3.6 Assigns application in teacher-made materials:** The teacher assigns application of a rule, skill, or strategy in teacher-made materials. |
| | | **3.7 Assigns application in real-world material:** The teacher assigns application of a rule, skill, or strategy in real-world materials such as books, telephone books, reading cereal boxes, following directions for putting models together, etc. |

| Observed | Not Observed | |
|---|---|---|
| | | **3.8 Helps with application:** The teacher helps students with problems related to application of a rule, skill, or strategy. |

How authentic was the material used for practice?

**4.0 Assessing Skill Performance:** This category includes everything a teacher does to assess and monitor skill performance.

| Observed | Not Observed | |
|---|---|---|
| | | **4.1 Checks assignment:** The teacher spends time with students in order to check assignments or checks assignments at desk while students complete something else. |
| | | **4.2 Assesses informally:** The teacher administers a teacher-made instrument to assess skill performance. |
| | | **4.3 Assesses formally:** The teacher administers a published instrument or instrument accompanying a basal program. |
| | | **4.4 Directs discussion:** The teacher directs open-ended discussion to obtain feedback from students on problems they are having with learning a rule, skill, or strategy. |
| | | **4.5 Asks questions about lesson:** During any part of skills lesson (teacher presentation, practice, or application), the teacher asks students questions related to what is being taught. |
| | | **4.6 Tells students what to know:** The teacher explicitly tells students answers to questions or information. |

**5.0 Other:** This category includes activities the teacher performs that are not related to the skills lesson.

| Observed | Not Observed | |
|---|---|---|
| | | **5.1 Demonstrates:** The teacher demonstrates how to do or use something unrelated to the skills lesson. |
| | | **5.2 Reads aloud:** The teacher reads aloud to students material that is not related to this lesson. |
| | | **5.3 Directs silent reading:** The teacher spends time directing silent reading that is not related to the lesson. |
| | | **5.4 Directs oral reading:** The teacher spends time directing oral reading that is not related to the lesson. |
| | | **5.5 Management and transition:** The teacher takes time to organize students, distribute materials, or shift from one activity to another. |
| | | **5.6 Noninstruction:** The teacher takes time to perform a noninstructional activity such as take up money or respond to a person coming to the door. |

**6.0. Debriefing**

At any time during the lesson, was there a debriefing on what was learned, how to use the skill outside the classroom, or what using the skill means?

How?

## Summary of Observation

Observing Reading Skills Instruction

School (Use a Code):

Observer:                               Date:

Summarize what you have learned from your observation.

# Observing Directed Reading Lesson

School (Use a Code):

Observer:                                    Date:

**I.  Pre-Reading Phase**

**1.0  Preparing for Reading:** This category includes what a teacher does to activate prior knowledge of student or to provide students with background information relevant to reading material. This category does not include the introduction of vocabulary, work attack skills, or purposes for reading.

| Observed | Not Observed | |
|---|---|---|
| | | **1.1 Asks for free recall:** The teacher asks students to think about and say or write down what they know about the material to be read or a related topic. |
| | | **1.2 Asks for word associations:** The teacher gives students a word or words about the topic to be read or a related topic and asks them to think about and say or write down what the words make them think of. |
| | | **1.3 Asks questions:** The teacher asks students questions related to what they might know about the topic to be read. |
| | | **1.4 Uses recognition statements:** The teacher gives students statements about the topic to be read or a related topic and asks students to tell what they know about the statements. |
| | | **1.5 Tells what to know:** The teacher tells students what they need to know about the topic to be read. |
| | | **1.6 Asks for predictions:** The teacher asks students to think about information, headings, characters, settings, and so on, and asks them to make predictions about the material to be read. |
| | | **1.7 Uses introductory material and media:** The teacher uses introductory paragraphs or other written material, diagrams, film, recordings, and the like to introduce the material to be read. |

If a strategy is being used, what is it?

**2.0 Introducing Vocabulary:** This category includes everything a teacher does to introduce vocabulary necessary for reading the material.

| Observed | Not Observed | |
|---|---|---|
| | | **2.1 Reviews previously learned vocabulary:** The teacher reviews earlier instruction on target vocabulary or other vocabulary. |
| | | **2.2 Uses definition:** The teacher gives students definitions for target vocabulary or asks them to use a dictionary or glossary to learn meaning. |
| | | **2.3 Uses personal definition:** The teacher elicits personal definitions for target vocabulary from students. |
| | | **2.4 Uses synonyms:** The teacher introduces target vocabulary by calling attention to or eliciting from students synonyms or words with similar meanings. |
| | | **2.5 Uses antonyms:** The teacher introduces vocabulary by calling attention to or eliciting from students antonyms associated with target vocabulary. |
| | | **2.6 Uses semantic association:** The teacher uses target vocabulary or other vocabulary as a stimulus for eliciting words students associate with target vocabulary. |
| | | **2.7 Uses semantic mapping:** The teacher categorizes or assists students in categorizing associated words to introduce target vocabulary. |
| | | **2.8 Uses semantic feature analysis:** The teacher introduces vocabulary by stressing the presence or absence of features usually possessed by words within categories. |

| Observed | Not Observed | |
|---|---|---|
| | | **2.9 Points out multiple meanings and technical use:** The teacher identifies for students and/or discusses the multiple meaning or technical use of vocabulary. |
| | | **2.10 Other:** The teacher introduces vocabulary with a strategy not identified in this category. |

If a strategy is being used, what is it?

**3.0 Introducing Word Attack Skills:** This category includes what a teacher does to teach or to call students' attention to word attack skills needed for reading the material. Thus, the category includes attention to phonics and structural analysis.

| Observed | Not Observed | |
|---|---|---|
| | | **3.1 Reviews previously learned word attack rule or skill:** The teacher reviews or calls attention to a previously learned word attack rule or skill. |
| | | **3.2 Teaches word attack rule or skill in isolation:** The teacher teaches a word attack rule or skill in the context of a single word or word lists. |
| | | **3.3 Teaches word attack rule or skill in context:** The teacher teaches a word attack rule or skill in context (words to which rule or skill applies presented with meaningful pictures or in sentences). |

If a strategy is being used, what is it?

**4.0 Developing Purpose for Reading:** This category includes what a teacher does in developing purposes for reading the material.

What was the purpose?

Was the purpose tied to the strategy for activating prior knowledge?

| Observed | Not Observed | |
|---|---|---|
| | | **4.1 Assigns reading without a purpose:** The teacher simply assigns material to be read (no questions to answer as a result of reading or no discussion of why to read). |
| | | **4.2 Assigns the purpose for reading:** The teacher assigns the purpose for reading, and no attempt is made to involve students in generating the purpose. |
| | | **4.3 Guides students in developing purpose for reading:** The teacher guides students in generating their own purpose for reading. |
| | | **4.4 Guides students in reading for student-teacher purpose:** The teacher directs discussion and peer interaction for developing student-teacher purposes for reading. |

## II. Reading Phase

**5.0 Guiding Silent Reading:** This category includes what a teacher does during the time students are reading.

| Observed | Not Observed | |
|---|---|---|
| | | **5.1 Helps with comprehension:** The teacher helps students overcome problems in understanding reading material (raises question, provides clues, etc.), and also, the teacher helps students determine the meaning of more than one word. |
| | | **5.2 Helps with word meaning:** The teacher helps students determine the meaning of single words. |
| | | **5.3 Helps with word attack:** The teacher provides students with assistance in decoding a word. |
| | | **5.4 Reviews comprehension instruction:** The teacher reviews previous instruction as a comprehension skill or strategy. |
| | | **5.5 Reviews vocabulary instruction:** The teacher reviews earlier instruction on vocabulary or word meaning. |
| | | **5.6 Reviews word attack instruction:** The teacher reviews previous instruction on phonics analysis or structural analysis. |
| | | **5.7 Assigns silent reading:** The teacher provides help to students by simply asking them to read or reread material. |

What strategy was used for getting help to students who needed help?

**6.0 Guided Rereading:** This category includes what a teacher does to engage students in rereading material that was read during silent reading.

| Observed | Not Observed | |
|---|---|---|
| | | **6.1 Assigns rereading with no purpose:** The teacher assigns rereading with no question to answer or topic to discuss. |
| | | **6.2 Assigns rereading in relation to original purpose for reading:** The teacher assigns rereading to pursue the original purpose for reading, to answer a question, or to discuss a topic related to the original purpose. |
| | | **6.3 Assigns rereading to answer a question:** The teacher assigns rereading for the purpose of answering a question unrelated to the original purpose. |
| | | **6.4 Directs discussion:** The teacher directs discussion related to the rereading of material. |

## III. Post-Reading Phase

**7.0 Guided Post-Reading Activity:** This category includes what a teacher does during the last phase of the directed reading activity. In general, this category will include assessment, review, and other activities directed related to material just read.

| Observed | Not Observed | |
|---|---|---|
| | | Did the teacher discuss the purpose for reading, first? How? [Describe.] |
| | | Did the teacher follow this routine, if questioning was the main strategy used? Asked questions based on the text first? Asked questions based on reader knowledge second? Asked questions about the author's craft last? |

| | | |
|---|---|---|
| | | Mixed the questions.<br>[Describe questioning] |
| | | **7.1 Asks questions:** The teacher asks students questions about material read, reading skills and strategies, and other information. |
| | | **7.2 Tells students what to do:** The teacher explicitly tells students answers to questions or information. |
| | | **7.3 Directs discussion:** The teacher directs open-ended discussion then engages students in interaction about material read. |
| | | **7.4 Assesses formally:** The teacher administers a published test to determine what students have learned during the reading activity. |
| | | **7.5 Assesses informally:** The teacher administers a teacher-made test or other informal instrument to determine what students have learned. |
| | | **7.6 Reviews comprehension instruction:** The teacher reviews previous instruction on a comprehension skill or strategy or reviews a comprehension skill or strategy used or discussed in this reading activity. |
| | | **7.7 Reviews vocabulary instruction:** The teacher reviews previous instruction on vocabulary or reviews vocabulary encountered or discussed in this reading activity. |
| | | **7.8 Reviews word attack instruction:** The teacher reviews previous instruction on word attack skills or reviews word attack skills used or discussed in this reading activity. |

**8.0 Guiding Follow-Up Activities:** This category includes what a teacher does to extend a directed reading activity. Included under this category are assignments made for the purpose of developing and pursuing reading interests, developing skills, and correlating other areas such as art with the reading activity.

| Observed | Not Observed | |
|---|---|---|
| | | **8.1 Makes assignment:** The teacher gives an assignment for the purpose of extending the reading activity. |
| | | **8.2 Helps with assignment:** The teacher provides help to students having problems with an assignment. |
| | | **8.3 Directs discussion:** The teacher spends time with students in order to check assignments or checks assignments at desk while students complete something else. |
| | | **8.4 Helps with application:** The teacher helps or directs students in the application of a rule, skill, or strategy. |
| | | **8.5 Reviews rules and applications:** The teacher reviews instruction on a rule or application. |

## IV. Other

**9.0 Other:** This category includes activities teacher performs that are not related to reading activities.

| Observed | Not Observed | |
|---|---|---|
| | | **9.1 Demonstrations:** The teacher demonstrates how to do or use something unrelated to the reading activity. |
| | | **9.2 Silent and oral reading:** The teacher spends time directing silent or oral reading that is not related to the reading activity. |

# Summary of Observation

Observing Dericted Reading Lesson

School (Use a Code):

Observer:                               Date:

Summarize what you have learned from your observation.

# Observing Instruction for English Language Learners

School (Use a Code):               Observer:

Grade:                          Date:

Curriculum Area:               Time In:            Time Out:

During this activity, you will be observing instruction provided to students whose native language is not English. There are a number of terms that are used in this area of education. Therefore, it will be beneficial for you to know the terms:

1. Teaching English to Speakers of Other Languages (TESOL) is the name of the field of study for teaching English to speakers of other languages.

2. English for Speakers of Other Languages (ESOL) refers to what the public schools call their program of language instruction for students who do not speak English.

3. Language 1 (L1) refers to one's native language, such as Spanish or English.

4. Language 2 (L2) refers to the language one learns after Language 1 (L1).

5. Limited English Proficient (LEP) is the term used in legislation related to ESOL.

6. English Language Learner (ELL) is the newest label used to refer to students whose native language is not English and who are receiving instruction in the public schools. This term is being used more frequently in professional literature and undergraduate textbooks. However, at this time, ELL is a term not frequently used in the public schools.

*Directions:* During this activity, you will be observing students engaged in instruction for ELLs. In some schools ELL instruction is provided by a regular classroom teacher who is bilingual. In other schools, it is provided by a special teacher who comes into the classroom. As you observe, check what you see and, when directed, provide evidence of the observation with descriptions of events and language used by the teacher and the students.

Use this space to make a rough sketch of the room in which instruction is conducted.

Who is responsible for the ELL instruction?

How frequently are students engaged in ELL instruction?

How long is the activity?

Provide a brief description of the lesson or activity observed.

**Teacher Use of L1 and L2**

When and why does the teacher use L1?     When and why does the teacher use L2?

**Student Use of L1 and L2**

When and why do students use L1?     When and why do students use L2?

How much time did students spend in different groupings for instruction?

- Individually _____
- Pairs or small groups _____
- Whole class _____

Describe the instructional activity.

---

Did the teacher identify who was going to be called on before he or she called on a student to answer a question or provide an explanation? Describe what you observed.

---

When the teacher invited students to answer questions, how much time did the students get before they were expected to respond? Do you think the time given was adequate or inadequate and why? Describe what you observed.

---

**The How and When of Feedback**        **Evidence**

Students receive feedback during:

- Speaking
- Writing
- Reading
- Immediately
- Later

Feedback is given in the following ways:
- Teacher provides cues and elaboration
- Teacher invites students to model for students
- Teacher invites students to freely discuss their response to music and level of play
- Teacher engages students in discussing errors
- Group discussion of how to perform better

How did students respond to feedback?
- Actively engaged
- Somewhat engaged
- Passively disengaged
- Not engaged at all

What was the students' level of engagement?
- Actively engaged
- Somewhat engaged
- Passively disengaged
- Not engaged at all

How would you judge this lesson?
- Lesson was too difficult for students
- Lesson was too easy for students
- Lesson was about the right level for students
- Most students were learning
- Some students would benefit from more individualized instruction
- Some students would benefit from more communicative interactions

Given your background in Language 1 and Language 2 learning thus far, what surprised you about the lesson, about the students' level of competence, and about the students' social behavior?

## Summary of Observation

Observing Instruction for English Language Learners

School (Use a Code):          Observer:

Grade:          Date:

Summarize what you have found out during your ELL observations.

## Observing Physical Education Instruction

| | |
|---|---|
| School (Use a Code): | Observer: |
| Grade: | Date: |
| Time In: | Time Out: |

*Directions:* During this activity, you will be observing students engaged in physical education activity. In the elementary grades, both classroom teachers and a physical education teacher may be responsible for this curriculum area. From middle school through high school, however, a physical education teacher is responsible. In addition, the curriculum may be more complex than you anticipate. The curriculum will include physical fitness, general and specific skills and concepts, organized sports, and leisure activities.

Along with observing, you will be gathering information. You may be able to gather the information before and after your observation. As you observe, check what you see and, when directed, provide evidence of the observation with descriptions of events and language used by the teacher and the students.

Make a rough sketch of the place where instruction is conducted.

Provide a brief description of the lesson or activity observed.

Who was responsible for instruction?

How frequently are students engaged in physical education?

How long is the activity?

How do students get to the place of the activity?

Was the activity coordinated with another course such as health?

What was the process for being excused from physical education?

**Observed instruction on the following skills and concepts:**       Evidence

- Warmup and stretching
- Moving
- Throwing
- Catching
- Kicking
- Striking
- Balance
- Agility
- Team sport
- Skills and concepts related to specific sports
- Lifetime activities

**Observed the physical fitness level of students being checked and progress monitored:**       Evidence

- Upper body strength
- Abdominal strength
- Endurance
- Flexibility of the lower back and hamstrings
- Cardiorespiratory endurance
- Monitoring of progress
- Reporting to parents

**Observed students engaged in:**       Evidence

- Drill and practice
- Demonstrations
- Team and group activity
- Presentation of information related to activity
- Instruction on rules and procedures
- Instruction on safety
- Instruction on how to use equipment

**Students received instruction:**       Evidence

- Individually
- In small groups
- Large groups

How did the teacher provide instruction (lecture, discussion, demonstration and modeling, explaining, etc.)?

How did the teacher provide students with feedback?

| How did the teacher engage in the activity? | Evidence |
|---|---|
| • Invited students to ask questions<br>• Invited students to interact with each other<br>• Invited students to demonstrate<br>• Invited students to freely discuss difficulty in performing some activities<br>• Invited students to discuss prior experiences with the activity<br>• Engaged students in discussion of how to perform better | |

What was the students' level of engagement?
- Actively engaged
- Somewhat engaged
- Passively disengaged
- Not engaged at all

How would you judge this lesson?
- Activity was too difficult for students
- Activity was too easy for students
- Activity was about the right level for students
- Most students understood the concepts and were mastering skills
- Some students would benefit from more instruction
- Some students would benefit from more practice

Given your background in physical education thus far, what surprised you about the lesson, about the students' level of competence, and about the students' social behavior?

# Summary of Observation

Observing Physical Education Instruction

School (Use a Code):

Observer:                                        Date:

Summarize what you have learned from your observation.

## Observing a Media Center

| | |
|---|---|
| School (Use a Code): | Observer: |
| Grade: | Date: |
| Curriculum Area: | Time In:       Time Out: |

Use the form below to conduct an observation of the phases of instruction found in a classroom.

*Directions:* During this activity, you will be observing activity in a school media center. Depending on the school, the media center may house the holdings of a traditional library, audiovisual equipment, computers, and multimedia. As you observe, check what you see and, when directed, provide evidence of the observation with descriptions of events and language used by the teacher and the students.

Make a rough sketch of the media center.

## Media Center Rules, Procedures, and Schedule

Evidence

- Are hours posted?
- What system is used to organize the main library collection?
- How are other equipment and multimedia organized?
- Are students allowed to frequently check out books and take them home?
- Are students allowed to check out equipment and multimedia to take home?

## Observing the Media Center Setting

Evidence

- Were tables and chairs an appropriate size?
- Were announcements and posters displayed on walls and doors?
- How many people worked in the media center and what did they do?
- How do students come and go from the media center (class, individual, etc.)?
- Does the media center have an open reading area?
- Does the media center have viewing and listening rooms?
- Does the media center have study or other work areas for students?

## Observing Student Supervision

Evidence

- Who brings the students to the media center?
- Does the adult who brings the students stay and supervise them?

| Library Collection | Evidence |
|---|---|

The library collection includes hardcopy materials, such as

- Fiction
- Nonfiction
- Magazines
- Materials in other languages
- Basic reference materials

| Electronic Resources | Evidence |
|---|---|

The media center has the following kinds of resources:

- Periodical guide
- Computers with search engines
- Periodical database
- Reference databases
- Newspapers and magazines
- Encyclopedias
- Thesauri
- Dictionaries
- Almanacs
- Atlases
- Other

| Equipment | Evidence |
|---|---|

Equipment includes:

- Computers
- VCRs
- Overhead projectors
- Tape recorders and players
- Video editors
- DVD players
- PC laptops
- LCD panels

- Camcorders
- Digital cameras
- Laminating tool
- Laser printer
- Poster printer

| Observing Student Behavior | Evidence |
|---|---|
| <ul><li>Were students allowed to interact among themselves?</li><li>Did students segregate themselves into groups or cliques? If so, how?</li><li>Did you observe any unacceptable behavior in the media center?</li></ul> | |

| Observing Learning Experiences | Evidence |
|---|---|
| <ul><li>Did you notice any instruction on how to use library materials, equipment, and other resources?</li><li>Did you notice any instruction about food groups, etc.?</li><li>Did you notice any special activity related to a particular topic being studied in class?</li></ul> | |

## Summary of Observation

Observing a Media Center

School (Use a Code):

Observer:                                    Date:

Summarize what you have learned from your observation.

# Observing a Technology Lab

School (Use a Code): _____ Observer: _____

Grade: _____ Date: _____

Curriculum Area: _____ Time In: _____ Time Out: _____

*Directions:* During this activity, you will be observing students using computers in a technology lab, and you will be collecting information about the computers in the lab. Thus, you may be able to collect some of the information before or after observing the students use the computers.

Make a rough sketch of the lab:



## Provide a Brief Description of the Activity You Observed

| General Lab Information | Your Comments |
|---|---|
| Who is in charge of the activity being observed?<br>• The classroom teacher<br>• The lab teacher | |
| How many computers are in the lab?<br>• One for the lab teacher<br>• One to ten computers<br>• Ten to twenty computers<br>• More than twenty computers | |

| General Lab Information | Your Comments |
|---|---|

How are the computers connected?

- Computers connected to a local network in school
- Only one computer providing Internet access
- More than one computer providing Internet access
- Only one computer connected to a printer
- More than one computer connected to a printer

How are the computers arranged in the lab?

- One computer per table
- Two or more computers per table
- Tables arranged in rows
- Monitors underneath table an viewed through a glass window
- Computers arranged so that students can attend to teacher
- Tables arranged as workstations with more than one computer per table

What peripherals are available for students to use?

- Printers
- CD towers
- Computer LCD panel or other projection devices
- Scanners
- Digital cameras
- CD and DVD writers
- Digital camcorders

The following activities seemed to be available to students:

- Word processing
- Creating spreadsheets

- Creating databases
- Drawing or painting with software
- Desktop publishing
- Multimedia publishing
- Image editing
- Using CD-ROM reference tools
- Using interactive laserdisc software
- Sending email
- Accessing the Internet
- Using web development tools
- Exploring programming languages
- Using math programs
- Using science programs
- Using English programs
- Using social studies programs
- Using foreign language programs
- Using typing tutors
- Exploring CAD-CAM and other industrial arts programs
- Using business programs

Lab Arrangement
- One student per computer
- One or two students per computer
- More than two students per computer

During the observed activity, computers were used for the following purposes:
- Obtaining information and ideas
- Analyzing information
- Building prior knowledge necessary for lessons, such as reading, math, etc.
- Mastering subject matter skills and knowledge
- Mastering computer and other technology skills
- Remedial work

| General Lab Information | Your Comments |
|---|---|

- Learning to work together
- Learning to work independently
- Making class presentations
- Communicating with others in class, another class, another school
- Exploring software
- Completing independent work

While engaged in computer activity students were:

- Looking up information
- Working on skills related to the curriculum, such as reading skills
- Writing, such stories, essays, or letters
- Creating illustrations or other art
- Playing games, such as *Carmen San Diego, Oregon Trails,* etc.
- Surfing the web
- Working on individual or group projects
- Taking tests

Students also worked on projects such as:

- Cross-school collaborative projects
- Independent projects
- Putting projects on the web
- Creating projects meeting their personal interests and goals

How did the teacher provide instruction (lecture, discussion, demonstration, explaining, etc.)? Provide a description that includes events and what was said.

How did the teacher provide students with feedback? Provide a description that includes events and what was said.

|  | Evidence |
|---|---|
| How did the teacher engage students in the activity? <br> • Students worked independently and already knew what to do <br> • Teacher gave the students a clear assignment with a purpose <br> • Instruction was mainly about how to use the computer <br> • Encouraged students to work independently <br> • Encouraged students to help each other | |
| What was the students' level of engagement? <br> • Actively engaged <br> • Somewhat engaged <br> • Passively disengaged <br> • Not engaged at all | Evidence |

Describe what led you to the decisions on engagement.

How would you judge this computer activity?

Given your background in using technology thus far, what surprised you about the lesson, about the students' level of competence, and about the students' social behavior?

## Summary of Observation

Observing a Technology Lab

School (Use a Code):

Observer:                                          Date:

Summarize what you have learned from your observation.

## Observing the Integration of Technology into Classroom Instruction

School (Use a Code):        Observer:

Grade:        Date:

Curriculum Area:        Time In:        Time Out:

*Directions:* During this activity, you will be observing students using computers and other technology in their classrooms, and you will be collecting information about the computers in the classroom. You may be able to collect some of the information before or after observing the students use computers.

Make a rough sketch of the classroom.

Provide a brief description of the instruction you observed, including the curriculum area, concepts, and skills, and materials used by the teacher.

| Consider the Following | Evidence and Comments |
|---|---|

**How many computers are in the classroom?**

- One computer under the control of the teacher
- No computers
- One computer
- One to three computers
- More than three computers

**How are the computers connected?**

- At least one computer is connected to a local network in the school
- At least one computer is dedicated to Internet access
- At least one computer is connected to a printer

**How are the computers arranged in the classroom?**

- One computer per desk
- Two or more computers on a desk
- Located in a corner
- Located along a wall
- Located near the center of the classroom

**How do students use the computers?**

- One student per computer
- One or two students per computer
- More than two students per computer

**For what purposes are the computers used?**

- Obtaining information and ideas
- Analyzing information

| Consider the Following | Evidence and Comments |
|---|---|

**For what purposes are the computers used?** *(cont.)*

- Building prior knowledge necessary for lessons, such as reading, math, etc.
- Mastering subject matter skills and knowledge
- Mastering computer and other technology skills
- Remedial work
- Learning to work together
- Learning to work independently
- Making class presentations
- Communicating with others in class, another class, another school, etc.
- Completing independent assignments

**What are the students doing at the computer?**

- Looking up information
- Working on skills related to the curriculum, such as reading skills
- Writing, such as stories, essays, or letters
- Creating illustrations or other art
- Playing games, such as *Carmen San Diego, Oregon Trails,* etc.
- Working on group projects
- Taking tests
- Surfing the web

| Consider the Following | Evidence and Comments |
|---|---|

How does the teacher engage the students in using computers?

- Students worked independently
- Teacher gave the students a clear assignment with a purpose
- Instruction was mainly about how to use the computer
- Encouraged students to work independently
- Encouraged students to help each other

How are the students engaged in the computer activity?

- Actively engaged
- Somewhat engaged
- Passively disengaged
- Not engaged at all

How would you judge the effectiveness of the activity and computer use?

- Activity was too difficult for students
- Activity was too easy for students
- Activity was at about the right level for students
- Most of the students understood the activity and learned subject matter or skills
- Some students understood the activity and learned subject matter or skills
- Some students did not understand the activity and did not learn subject matter or skills
- Most of the students did not understand the activity and did not learn subject matter or skills

To what extent do you feel the use of technology in this activity increased students' level of understanding of the subject matter and increased their skill in using the technology?

What surprised you most about the use of technology in this classroom and the students' skill with it?

Given what you have been learning about technology in your teacher preparation program and what you have observed in this classroom, how do you feel about what you know and what you need to learn?

## Summary of Observation

Observing the Integration of Technology into Classroom Instruction

School (Use a Code):

Observer:                                    Date:

Summarize what you have learned from your observation.

# Observing Art Instruction

School (Use a Code): _____ Observer: _____

Grade: _____ Date: _____

Time In: _____ Time Out: _____

*Directions:* During this activity, you will be observing students engaged in art instruction. Students who participate in art instruction are likely to participate in whole class art activities or studio projects. An art lesson will also vary according to the level of student accomplishment, methods, and media. Depending on the particular class you observe, you will probably have an opportunity to observe instruction at the beginner, immediate, and accomplished levels. As you observe, check what you see and, when directed, provide evidence of the observation with descriptions of events and language used by the teacher and the students.

Many art classes may engage students in the use of different kinds of media. Depending on the kind of media, there are potential hazards. For example, some materials are highly flammable. Other materials may be potentially dangerous to students with certain allergies. Safety is a constant environmental issue. Rules and regulations must be taken seriously. Thus, one section of your observation will deal with these issues.

Make a rough sketch of the room in which instruction is conducted.

Observed instruction on the following content and concepts:

List the art methods students were exploring:

How did you recognize these methods?

List the materials students were using:

How were the materials being used?

How did the teacher provide instruction (lecture, discussion, demonstration, explaining, etc.)?

How did the teacher provide students with feedback?

| How did the teacher engage students in the activity? | Evidence |
|---|---|
| • Invited students to ask questions<br>• Invited students to interact with each other<br>• Invited students to demonstrate<br>• Invited students to freely discuss their response to methods and media<br>• Engaged students in discussing their ideas, interpretations, and responses to art<br>• Engaged students in discussion of how to perform better | |
| What was the students' level of engagement? | Evidence |
| • Actively engaged<br>• Somewhat engaged<br>• Passively disengaged<br>• Not engaged at all | |
| How would you judge this lesson? | Evidence |
| • Lesson was too difficult for students<br>• Lesson was too easy for students<br>• Lesson was about the right level for students<br>• Some students would benefit from more feedback and instruction<br>• Some students would benefit from more practice | |

| Considering the following: | Evidence |
| --- | --- |
| • Cleanliness of classroom, warnings of hazards, rules and regulations, lighting, and ventilation<br><br>• Storage, distribution, and care of tools and media<br><br>• Potential problems related to allergies, chemical sensitivities, or respiratory problems and exposure to materials<br><br>• Student knowledge about procedures for using tools and media | |

## Summary of Observation

Observing Art Instruction

School (Use a Code):

Observer:                                    Date:

Summarize what you have learned from your observation.

## Observing Band Instruction

School (Use a Code): _____     Observer: _____

Grade: _____     Date: _____

Time In: _____     Time Out: _____

*Directions:* During this activity, you will be observing students engaged in band instruction. Students who participate in this instruction are likely to participate in other music activities, such as the Marching Band, the Pep Band, and the Jazz Band, along with participation in solo and ensemble performances. Depending on the particular class you observe, you will probably have an opportunity to observe instruction at the beginner, immediate, and accomplished levels of the band program. The content, concepts, and instructional activities that you might observe will, therefore, have great breadth and depth.

As you observe, check what you see and, when directed, provide evidence of the observation with descriptions of events and language used by the teacher and the students.

Make a rough sketch of the room in which instruction is conducted:

## Provide a Brief Description of the Lesson or Activity Observed

| Observed Students Engaged in Learning Activities Related to (circle any bullets): | Your Comments |
| --- | --- |

- Rhythm patterns, such as perception of two-, three-, and four-unit meters independently, and in group ensemble
- Basic note reading techniques
- Tone production on wind instruments
- Tone production on brass instruments
- Tone production on percussion instruments
- Tone production on string instruments
- Rhythmic sight-reading patterns
- Playing, at sight and independently, musical passages in low, middle, and upper registers
- Use and care of instruments
- Playing in tune
- Performing duple- and triple-meter music
- Emphasizing measure unit with accent
- Following critical markings of musical scores
- Performing major and minor scales independently
- Responding correctly to melodic and rhythmic aural dictation exercises
- Basics of electronic music
- Sight-reading exercises
- Aural dictation and ear training
- Improvising to a given chord progression

- Playing in tune
- Playing a wide variety of concert and jazz repertoire
- Performing as soloist and in small and large group ensembles

Students Received Instruction:
- Individually
- In ensembles
- As whole group

How did the teacher provide instruction (lecture, discussion, demonstration, explaining, etc.)?

How did the teacher provide students with feedback?

How did the teacher engage students in the activity? (circle appropriate bullets)         Evidence
- Invited students to ask questions
- Invited students to interact with each other
- Invited students to freely discuss their response to music and performance
- Engaged students in discussing their ideas and interpretations of music
- Engaged students in discussion of how to perform better

| What was the students' level of engagement? | Evidence |
|---|---|
| • Engaged in discussing their ideas and interpretations of music<br>• Actively engaged<br>• Somewhat engaged<br>• Passively disengaged<br>• Not engaged at all | |
| How would you judge this lesson? | Evidence |
| • Lesson was too difficult for students<br>• Lesson was too easy for students<br>• Lesson was about the right level for students<br>• Most students understood the content and were mastering skills<br>• Some students would benefit from more instruction<br>• Some students would benefit from more practice | |

## Summary of Observation

Observing Band Instruction

School (Use a Code):

Observer:                                    Date:

Summarize what you have learned from your observation.

## Observing a Cafeteria

School (Use a Code):                 Observer:

Grade:                                 Date:

Time In:                            Time Out:

*Directions:* During this activity, you will be observing activity in the school cafeteria. School cafeterias differ in size and the number. You may even notice that some of the cafeteria staff have worked at their jobs for a long time. If you have time, you might find having lunch in the cafeteria to be an informative experience.

As you observe, check what you see and, when directed, provide evidence of the observation with descriptions of events and language used by teachers and students.

Make a rough sketch of the cafeteria you are observing:

| Cafeteria Rules, Procedures, and Schedule | Evidence |
| --- | --- |
| • Was the cafeteria used for purposes other than providing lunch, such as a place for students before and after school?<br><br>• How many meals did the cafeteria serve each day?<br><br>• What was the grade-level schedule for going to the cafeteria?<br><br>• How long did students have for lunch?<br><br>• Did students pay for lunch in the classroom or in the cafeteria?<br><br>• If students brought a prepared lunch from home, what did they do?<br><br>• Were students who receive a free lunch noticed easily?<br><br>• Could students read or study in the cafeteria?<br><br>• Was there a special table for teachers and administrators? Are visitors allowed in the cafeteria? | |

| Observing the Cafeteria Setting | Evidence |
| --- | --- |
| • Were tables and chairs an appropriate size?<br><br>• Were announcements and posters displayed on walls and doors?<br><br>• What was the noise level?<br><br>• Was the lunch period rushed or unrushed?<br><br>• Was the cafeteria floor and furniture free of spills and bits of trash and food?<br><br>• How many people worked in the cafeteria? | |

## Observing Student Supervision                    Evidence

- Who brought the students to the cafeteria?
- Did the adult who brought the students sit with them and eat lunch?
- Were the students monitored by an adult as they ate lunch?
- Was there a flow of conversation between adults and students?

## Observing Hygiene                    Evidence

- Did students have an opportunity to wash their hands before eating?
- Did students have an opportunity to brush their teeth after eating?

## Observing Student Behavior                    Evidence

- Were students allowed to interact among themselves?
- Did students segregate themselves into groups or cliques? If so, how?
- Did you observe any unacceptable behavior in the cafeteria?

- Did you notice any instruction on how to use knives, spoons, forks, or napkins?
- Did you notice any discussion of manners?
- Did you notice any instruction about food groups, etc.?
- Did you notice any special activity related to a particular food being served or a topic being studied in class?
- Do you think students had an opportunity to learn any knowledge or skills that would enable them to participate in dining at a public restaurant?

If you had lunch in the cafeteria, how do you rate the quality of the lunch served? Did you find lunch to be a pleasant experience? Why? Why not?

## Summary of Observation

Observing a Cafeteria

School (Use a Code):

Observer:                                          Date:

Summarize what you have learned from your observation.

# Observing in a Museum, Exploratorium, Planetarium, or Exhibition

School (Use a Code):            Observer:

Grade:            Date:

Curriculum Area:            Time In:            Time Out:

*Directions:* Your observation should take approximately spend 30-45 minutes.

- Try to observe more than one exhibit.
- Try to observe in different locations.
- Try to select exhibits or displays that a lot of children spend a lot of time with and observe whoever arrives during your time.
- Individuals or groups generally do not spend a great deal of time at one exhibit. Be prepared to observe a number of different groups and episodes.
- Be prepared to observe children and adults who come together.
- If possible, try to get close enough to hear what is said. If you can, write down segments of dialogue from each episode you observe.

## Recording the Observation

- Write down as much as you can about what is going on in each episode or activity. Each episode should include the number of minutes the individual or group stayed and who was in the group (number of children, number of adults). Focus on:
  - What role does each adult and child play?
  - Who initiates the interactions? (Did the child ask questions? What kind of information did the adult provide?)
  - What do you think the children that you observed learned? Why or why not?

## Writing up the Observation

- After your observation, review your notes. Use these notes and what you can remember.

- You will have observed a number of different episodes. Don't try to write up everything that you observed. Step back and think about what you observed.

- You might decide to provide a broad description of what you observed. Pick two or more themes or patterns that occurred repeatedly in different episodes at the same exhibit. What about the exhibit seemed to cause these similarities across different groups? What do these common themes or patterns reveal about the exhibit?

- You might decide to provide an in-depth approach or description of what you observed. Select two or more episodes that contain interactions between two or more same-age peers or children with adults. Your episodes should contain the dialogue that occurred in the episodes. In contrast to a broad description, you should say more about the group of participants and what learning took place. You should also describe what the interactions among the participants reveal about the exhibit.

- Interpret your observation by drawing on what you have read in class and class discussion.

## Summary of Observation

Observing in a Museum, Exploratorium, Planetarium, or Exhibition

School (Use a Code):

Observer:                          Date:

Summarize what you have learned from your observation.

# Observing School-Related Meetings

| School (Use a Code): | Observer: | |
| --- | --- | --- |
| Grade: | Date: | |
| Curriculum Area: | Time In: | Time Out: |

Teachers, administrators, and staff engage in many activities that support classroom instruction, the main activity of education. Among these activities are school board meetings, faculty meetings, departmental meetings, grade-level meetings, teacher team meetings, staffing meetings for special needs students, Parent Teacher Organization meetings, professional development meetings, and more. The purpose of this observation activity is to engage you in attending a meeting that your instructor assigns, observing the meeting, and writing a summary of what happened.

*Directions:* You have probably always been a participant in a meeting rather than an observer. The purpose of the six steps below is to help you direct your attention to elements of a meeting that you might not otherwise notice. Before the meeting, review these steps. As the meeting convenes and progresses, jot down as many notes as you can that are relevant to each step. If the meeting moves along quickly, you may have to take notes quickly and then go back and organize them according to the steps. Finally, you should write a summary of the meeting based on your notes.

| Step One: Determining the Purpose or Topic | Evidence |
| --- | --- |
| • How would you define the central topics of the meeting? <br> • For each topic, describe the topic, central issue, problem, task, or goal. | |

| Step Two: Identifying the Outcomes | Evidence |
| --- | --- |
| • As the meeting is conducted, try to determine the outcome of the discussion of each topic. It might be helpful to create a sequence for how each topic was discussed and a decision made. | |

| Step 3: Noticing Disturbances | Evidence |
|---|---|
| • Confusion: A series of interruptions where speakers speak out of turn or on top of each other.<br><br>• Disagreement: A point where a speaker openly questions or challenges another speaker's statement or argument, or offers an argument as an alternative.<br><br>• What was the issue and what were the different perspectives offered by each participant?<br><br>• How did the chairperson, leader, or group deal with the disturbance? For example, did the meeting come to a halt? Were the participants silenced, or did the participants try to develop a solution? | |
| Step Four: Offering Help to Solve Issues and Problems | Evidence |
| • Identify all sequences in the meeting where participants offer helpful suggestions and ideas that were clearly intended to solve a problem.<br><br>• What was the issue and what were the different perspectives offered by each participant?<br><br>• How did the chairperson, leader, or group react to the suggestions— for example, were suggestions discussed when they were offered or later, were the suggestions ignored, or did the participants decide to accept the suggestions?<br><br>• Did anything happen during this sequence; if so, what happened and when? | |

| Step Five: Noting Interactions | Evidence |
|---|---|
| • Identify all the sequences in the meeting where participants ask for clarification or information to help them better understand the meeting, problems, suggestions, etc.<br><br>• How did the chairperson, leader, or group react to the request? For example, was the request ignored, was information given by the chairperson, or did the participants offer information? | |

| Step Six: Try to identify how the group used the tools brought to the meeting: | Evidence |
|---|---|
| • Describe how written documents, agendas, and notes were used.<br><br>• Describe how records were used.<br><br>• Describe how pictures, drawings, and other representations were used.<br><br>• Describe how minutes or other summaries containing earlier decisions were used. | |

# Summary of Observation

Observing School-Related Meetings

School (Use a Code):

Observer: Date:

What kind of meeting did you attend?

- School board
- Parent Teacher Organization
- Faculty
- Grade level
- Departmental
- Curriculum
- Professional development
- Student problem
- Other (specify)

## Points to Consider in Writing Your Summary

Was this a regularly scheduled meeting or a specially called meeting?

Who attended the meeting? Members? Guests?

Did you notice whether key members of the meeting were absent? If so, who?

Was the meeting area used for other purposes?

_____

Did participants refer to the notes and other items (notes, plans, test data summaries of previous meetings, records) they brought to the meeting? If so, how?

_____

Who participated in the meeting? What was each one's position (teacher, parent, etc.)? Did they represent others, such as teachers, community, or business?

_____

What was the purpose of the meeting? Did the meeting have an agenda? If so, what was the agenda?

_____

How did the meeting progress (agenda was followed, open-ended, etc.)?

_____

How did participants get to speak (called on, volunteered, took turns, raised their hand to be acknowledged)?

What was the nature of the discussion? Were there arguments and tensions? If so, why?

How did the discussion go? Who did you think were the most influential participants and why?

How did the meeting close?
- What plans were made for the next meeting?
- How did the participants decide what needed to be done for the next meeting?
- Did they volunteer for tasks or were tasks assigned to individuals?

How did the participants reach a consensus?

# PART III
...........................

# Interview Instruments

**P**art III of this book provides interview schedules to use in your fieldwork.

Like the observation schedules in Part II, these interview schedules do not need to be followed slavishly. Instead, use them as you see fit. Adapt and modify them in ways that work best for your work in the field.

## Learning about a Teacher as an Individual

*Directions:* Use the questions below to conduct an interview with a teacher. Make sure that you have the signed permission of the teacher before you begin your interview. In addition to taking notes, you may want to tape record your interview and transcribe it.

| | |
|---|---|
| School (Use a Code): | Interviewer: |
| Grade: | Date: |
| Curriculum Area: | Time In:       Time Out: |
| Teacher Name: | |
| Teacher Signature: | |

1. Why did you choose a career in teaching? Did you consider other career choices? If so, what?

2. What are/were your mother's and father's occupations? How did family and friends react to your decision to teach?

3. How long have you been in the classroom? How long do you plan to teach?

4. What is your educational background? What kinds of elementary and secondary schools did you attend? What kind of a college or university did you attend?

5. Were there any teachers who influenced your decision to teach or your teaching style?

6. What are you trying most to achieve with students? What goals do you hold for students? What methods and strategies do you use to achieve these goals?

7. What is your greatest satisfaction in teaching?

8. What is your greatest frustration in teaching?

9. To what degree do you think the context of the school affects what you do in the classroom?

10. If you had to do it all over again, would teaching still be your career choice? If yes, why? If no, why not?

# Learning about a School Administrator as an Individual

*Directions:* Use the questions below to conduct an interview with a school administrator. Make sure that you have the signed permission of the administrator before you begin your interview. In addition to taking notes you may want to tape record your interview and transcribe it.

| | |
|---|---|
| School (Use a Code): | Interviewer: |
| Grade: | Date: |
| Curriculum Area: | Time In: Time Out: |

Administrator Name:

Administrator Signature:

1. Why did you choose a career in administration? Did you consider other career choices? If so, what?

2. What are/were your mother's and father's occupations? How did family and friends react to your decision to enter the field of education?

3. How long have you been working in schools?

4. What is your educational background? What kinds of elementary and secondary schools did you attend? What kind of a college or university did you attend?

5. Were there any administrators who influenced your decision to become an administrator or your administrative style?

6. What are you trying most to achieve with students? What goals do you hold for students? What methods and strategies do you use to achieve these goals?

7. What is your greatest satisfaction as an administrator?

8. What is your greatest frustration as an administrator?

9. To what degree do you think the context of the school affects what you do as an administrator?

10. If you had to do it all over again, would administration still be your career choice? If yes, why? If no, why?

## Interviewing a Student (Understanding How Well Students Understand Instruction)

| | |
|---|---|
| School (Use a Code): | Observer: |
| Grade: | Date: |
| Curriculum Area: | Time In:      Time Out: |

To what extent do students understand the instruction in which they are engaged? Probably no two students understand and interpret the instruction in which they are engaged in the same way. Similarly, students develop different understandings of subject matter areas, such as reading, math, science, history, biology, and the like. The purpose of this interview is for you to gain insight into students' understanding of what they are learning and why.

*Directions:* Depending on how much time you have, you might ask the teacher to identify three students who are achieving at different levels. You might use the following script with the students: I am learning to teach. One of my assignments in my class is to find out what students think about what they are learning in school. Today, I want you to tell me about what you are learning in (name the subject matter area). So, I want you to think about your lesson in (name the subject matter area).

### I. Understanding Instruction

1. What does your teacher do to get you ready for a lesson?

2. What was the lesson about today? What can you tell me about what you were learning?

3. What was easy for you in the lesson?

4. What was hard for you in the lesson?

5. What would you tell your best friend you learned in the lesson today?

6. Who helps you the most when you don't understand the lesson or when you have a problem with it? What kind of help does the person usually give you?

7. How do you think what you learned in the lesson today could be used in another lesson, like (give the names of two subject matter areas)?

8. How do you think you could use what you learned in the lesson today outside of school?

## II. Using Learning Strategies

1. When you do not understand the lesson or it gets hard for you, what do you do?

2. Can you give me some examples of how you help yourself? What little tricks do you use?

3. If your best friend needed help in today's lesson, what would you tell him or her to do?

### III. Relations among Skills and Subject Matter They Are Learning

1. Can you tell me how what you learned in today's lesson is like what you learned in another lesson, like (name two or more subject matter areas)?

2. Can you tell me how what you learned in today's lesson is different from what you learned in another lesson, like (name two or more subject matter areas)?

### IV. Evaluation of Their Own Progress

1. What is your favorite school subject?

2. How much do you think you have you learned about it?

3. What are you good at in school? How do you know you are good at it?

4. What are you not good at in school? How do you know?

5. Do your parents know how much you are learning in school? How do they find out?

## V. Summarizing Your Interview.

Before you summarize your interview, here are a few points for you to consider.

1. What surprised you the most about how the student responded?

2. How would you describe what the students know and understand about what they are learning?

3. If you interviewed more than one student, how would you describe the major similarities and differences between them?

4. Based on this interview, what questions would you like discussed in your class?

# APPENDIX
......................................

# A Three-Step Model for Conducting Classroom Observations, Interviews, and Participation in Classroom Activity

**I**n this section we provide a three-step model for conducting classroom observations, interviews, and participation in classroom activity. It should be adapted and used according to your needs. It can be easily integrated into the materials previously introduced in this book.

The goal for engaging in field experiences such as observation and participation is not simply to have the experience and tell about it in class. Rather, the goal is to have beginning teachers develop a meaningful professional knowledge base by engaging in a process of inquiry on concepts, principles, or topics and taking steps to transform the results into personal knowledge and understanding for practice as a professional. The framework outlined below is one way to organize instruction to accomplish this goal. It involves three steps:

1. Making knowledge public
2. Building anchors
3. Making connections and objectifying

# A Three-Step Instructional Framework for Conducting Classroom Observations and Interviews

### Step 1: Making Knowledge Public

| Activating Prior Knowledge | Organizing Prior Knowledge | Setting Purpose |
|---|---|---|

1. Beginning teacher/observers complete a pre-free write (Elbow, 1981) on the principle, concept, or topic to be studied.

2. Beginning teacher/observers engage in activities that activate and organize their prior knowledge about the principle, concept, or topic, including:

   a. Semantic map (Heimlich & Pittleman, 1986)

   b. K-W-L procedure (Ogle, 1986)

   c. Anticipation guide (Readence, Bean, & Baldwin, 1989)

   d. PREP (Langer, 1981)

3. Beginning teacher/observers and their instructor organize prior knowledge into a visual display (map, chart, etc.) and discuss its organization and what they might want to learn or make predictions about what they expect to learn.

4. Beginning teacher/observers are given a reading or viewing assignment with the purpose of either updating their knowledge or confirming their predictions.

### Step 2: Building Anchors

| Reading and Viewing | Reformulating, Confirming, and Integrating | Planning Inquiry |
|---|---|---|

1. Beginning teacher/observers update their knowledge or confirm predictions by reading a text or viewing a video.

2. Beginning teacher/observers update their visual display and discuss how what they knew has changed. Students discuss the accuracy of their predictions and evidence used to determine accuracy.

3. Beginning teacher/observers and their instructor outline what they want to learn about the principle, concept, or topic as they observe or participate in the field.

### Step 3: Making Connections and Objectifying

| Participating, Observing, and Inquiring | Formulating and Communicating | Constructing Knowledge and Developing Understanding |
| --- | --- | --- |

1. Beginning teacher/observers observe and participate in the field to inquire on the meaning of the principle, concept, or topic.

2. Beginning teacher/observers formulate and write field notes on their observation and participation.

3. Beginning teacher/observers discuss field notes in class. The aim is to convert experiences into meaning and knowledge about the principle, concept, or topic and to index the results to meaning making resources in the observed or participatory setting.

4. Beginning teacher/observers relate the discussion to the purpose of their inquiry and revisit the visual display of their prior knowledge, update it, and discuss how it has changed or discuss new evidence supporting confirmation or disconfirmation of their prediction.

5. Instructor and class objectify events that were observed and reported in field notes.

6. Beginning teacher/observers reflect on what has been learned, what it means, and discuss how it is related to future courses and teaching.

7. Beginning teacher/observers complete a post-free write on the principle, concept, or topic studied.

### STEP ONE

*Making Knowledge Public* promotes making what the class knows about a topic both public and visible. Theoretical knowledge systems and their meanings need to be made obvious to beginning teacher/observers so that they can see how concepts fit together and how they are interpreted. Instruction begins with having them complete a *Quick Write* to provide a measure of their prior knowledge about a topic or concept. Next, an instructional strategy is used to activate, organize, and display the collective prior knowledge of the beginning teacher. Then a purpose compatible with the instructional strategy is introduced for a reading or viewing assignment.

## STEP TWO

The process of *Building Anchors* follows the completion of the reading or viewing assignments. Following the reading or viewing assignment, the instructor and students add information to their visual display or information related to predictions. This information is reorganized and becomes a conceptual anchor on which to connect new information during observation and participation. The purpose of *Building Anchors* is to update and reorganize beginning teacher/observers' knowledge into a conceptual anchor, following completion of the reading or viewing assignment. The anchor provides a framework for building further knowledge through the observation and interview process that can be integrated with new information and prior knowledge, thus providing a framework for participating, observing, and inquiring on concepts during fieldwork.

## STEP THREE

The purpose of *Making Connections and Objectifying* is to assist beginning teacher/observers in applying the new learning from Phases One and Two to field experiences. The writing of field notes is a tool to engage beginning teacher/observers in inquiring and reflecting on course content as it relates to field experiences. Field notes also focus their attention on events, such as how teachers teach, what is taught, how children learn, what they learn, and how teachers and children use what they know in the setting being observed. The in-class discussion during this step always begins with the purpose of the observation, participation, and inquiry by returning to Phase Two. Discussions of field notes assist beginning teacher/observers in confronting and subjecting their preconceptions to critical analysis. Over time, they begin to use concepts with increasing frequency to mediate the conversion of content and experiences into knowledge and to formulate and communicate in writing and discussion. Instruction always ends with a debriefing on what has been learned, what it means, and how it is related to future courses and teaching performance. Finally, another free write is administered to obtain information for evaluating what has been learned.

The above model can be used with any of the observation, interview, or participation forms included in this book. We believe it is an extremely useful way for beginning teacher/observers to organize and integrate the results from conducting field-based interviews and observations.

This model can be used formally or informally. It is only a suggested approach and can be modified or disregarded according to the needs of the instructor.

# Bibliography

Benne, K. (1943). *A conception of authority*. New York: Teachers College, Columbia University Bureau of Publications.

Britzman, D. P. (1986). Cultural myths in the making of a teacher: Biography and social structure in teacher education. *Harvard Educational Review, 56*(4), 442–456.

Carpenter, T., Fennema, E., Peterson, P., & Carey, D. (1988). Teachers' pedagogical content knowledge of students' problem-solving in elementary arithmetic. *Journal for Research in Mathematics Education, 19,* 385–401.

Cohen, D., & Ball, D. (1990). Policy and practice: An overview. *Educational Evaluation and Policy Analysis, 12*(3), 347–353.

Durkin, D. (1978–79). What classroom observations reveal about reading comprehension instruction. *Reading Research Quarterly, 14*(4), 481–533.

Elbow, P. (1981). *Writing with power*. New York: Oxford University Press.

Giroux, Henry A. (1992). *Border crossings: Cultural workers and the politics of education*. New York: Routledge.

Giroux, Henry A. (1994). *Disturbing pleasures: Learning popular culture*. New York: Routledge.

Giroux, Henry A. (1997). *Pedagogy and the politics of hope: Theory, culture, and schooling*. Boulder, CO: Westview Press.

Goodwin, C. (1994). Professional vision. *American Anthropologist, 96*(3), 606–633.

Grossman, P., Valencia, S., & Thompson, C. (2000, April). *District policy as a context for learning to teach*. Paper presented at the Annual Meeting of the American Educational Research Association at New Orleans.

Heimlich, J. E., & Pittelman, S. D. (1986). *Semantic mapping: Classroom applications*. Newark, DE: International Reading Association.

Knapp, M., Gallucci, C., & Markholt, A. (2001). *Constructing a coherent teaching policy environment in an urban sub-district*. Paper presented at the Annual Meeting of the American Educational Research Association at New Orleans.

Langer, J. (1981). From theory to practice: A prereading plan. *Journal of Reading, 25,* 152–156.

McLaughlin, M. W., & Talbert, J. E. (1993). *Contests that matter for teaching and learning: Strategic opportunities for meeting the nation's educational goals*. Stanford, CA: Center for Research on the Context of Secondary School Teaching, Stanford University. (ERIC Document Reproduction Service No. ED 357 023)

Ogle, D. (1986). K-W-L: A teaching model that develops active reading of expository text. *The Reading Teacher, 39,* 564–567.

Pajares, M. F. (1992). Teachers' beliefs and educational research: Cleaning up a messy construct. *Review of Educational Research, 62,* 307–332.

Ratekin, N., Simpson, M. L., Alvermann, D. E., & Dishner, E. K. (1985). Why teachers resist content reading instruction. *Journal of Reading, 28,* 432–437.

Readence, J. E., Bean, T. W., & Baldwin, R. S. (1989). *Content area reading: An integrated approach* (3rd ed.). Dubuque, IA: Kendall/Hunt.

Schön, D. A. (1987). *Educating the reflective practitioner: Toward a new design for teaching and learning in the professions.* San Francisco: Jossey-Bass.

Smith, F. R., & Feathers, K. M. (1983). Teacher and student perceptions of content area reading. *Journal of Reading, 1,* 344–354.

Stodolsky, S. S., Ferguson, T. L., & Wimpelberg, K. (1981). The recitation persists, but what does it look like? *Journal of Curriculum Studies, 12,* 121–130.

Thompson, A. G. (1984). The relationship of teachers' conceptions of mathematical teaching to instructional practice. *Educational Studies in Mathematics, 15,* 105–127.